STORIES FOR A WINTER'S NIGHT

STORIES FOR A
WINTER'S NIGHT
SHORT FICTION BY NATIVE AMERICANS

EDITED BY
MAURICE KENNY

INTRODUCTION BY
A. LAVONNE RUOFF

WHITE PINE PRESS · BUFFALO, NEW YORK

WHITE PINE PRESS
P.O. Box 236, Buffalo, New York 14201

Acknowledgments: "Che," by Anna Lee Walters first appeared in *Talking Indian*, Firebrand Books, Ithaca, N.Y. Copyright ©1992 by Ana Lee Walters. "The Derelict" by E. Pauline Johnson appeared in *The Moccasin Maker*, A. Lavonne Brown Ruoff, ed., University of Arizona Press. "Train Time" by D'Arcy McNickle appeared in *The Hawk is Hungry*, University of Arizona Press. "Haksod" by John Mohawk first appeared in *Iroquois Voices, Iroquois Visions*, Bertha Rogers, ed., Bright Hill Press. "Needles" by Ray Fadden and "The Car Wreck" by Dwayne Leslie Bowen appeared in *New Voices from the Longhouse*, Joseph Bruchac, ed., Greenfield Review Press. "The Panther Waits" by Simon J. Ortiz appeared in *Fightin': New and Collected Stories*, Thunder's Mouth Press, 1985, and is used by permission of the author. "Brewing Trouble" by Kimberly Blaeser first appeared in *Callaloo* and is reprinted by permission of the author. Acknowledgments continue on page 206.

Publication of this book was made possible, in part,
with public funds from the New York State Council on the Arts, a state agency,
and by a grant from the Lannan Foundation.

Cover art: Rokwaho

Printed and bound in the United States of America

1 3 5 7 9 10 8 6 4 2

Library of Congress Cataloging-in-Publication Data
Stories for a winter's night : short fiction by Native Americans /
edited by Maurice Kenny ; introduction by A. LaVonne Ruoff
    p. cm.
ISBN 1-877727-96-2 (alk. paper)
I. Short stories, American—Indian authors. 2. Indians of North America—Fiction.
3. American fiction—20th century. I. Kenny, Maurice, 1929-
PS508.I5 S76 2000
813'.0108897—dc2163   99-088311

CONTENTS

Notes on Tribal Designations
The Ojibwe: The current official name of the groups in Minnesota, Wisconsin, and Michigan is *Ojibwe* with an *e* rather thay an *a* or *ay*.

Ashshinabe, Chippewa, Ojibway, Ojibwa, and Ojibwe all refer to the same group.

The official name of the nation formerly called Creek is now Muscogee-Creek.

The tribe formerly referred to as Flathead is now Condfederated Salish-Koutennai Tribes.

In memory of my sister Mary,
who passed into the spirit world May 1997
but who told me many stories
when I was a young boy

. . .

and in memory of
Diane Decorah
Lorne Simon
Fred Hoch
Allen Ginsberg
Denise Levertov
Olga Cabral

. . .

and for the late David Fisher
writer, friend

. . .

and to the Adironaack Mountains
who hold mysteries
yet tell stories, too,
if you listen

. . .

and for Tony Waickman,
who has kept me alive these years
and to Cliff Tafzou
for the new road

PREFACE

"I grew up at Laguna listening, and I hear the ancient stories, I hear them very clearly in the stories we are telling
right now. Most important, I feel the power which the stories still have, to bring us together, especially when there
is loss and grief."

—Leslie Marmon Silko
Storyteller

Stories are for winter nights when the lodge is warm from a
good wood fire and safe from whatever predator—human, animal or spirit. Stories are meant to entertain, but tales are also
used as teaching tools. Winter nights in the lodge become class-
room nights as the traditional storyteller spins and weaves
excitement and quite possibly a humanistic leasson into tales of
valor; discovery; ghostly visitations; travels; war; strawberry or
blackberry pickings; love, of course; birth and death, naturally;
and stories of natural phenomenon, such as how the "great dip-
per" came into the sky, why wolves are considered brothers,
where medicine came from, why grass is green, how the buffalo
got its horns. Stories were told while women sewed, men fluted
arrowheads, and children curled into questions, breaking into

---

smiles at the answers.

A story, a fiction, is something from the imagination, quite possibly a lie or something developed from gossip in the berry patch or cornfield. Fiction is the opposite of fact and yet fact must be the basis for fictionalizing, telling tales. Consequently, fiction becomes fact, and story becomes lesson.

This collection begins with a traditional Cheyenne story, "The Stolen Girl," which offers an explanation of how rats get into a village and was meant to frighten young girls into staying safely in the tipi and not be taken in by strangers. Peter Blue Cloud, whose humorous stories always have a point, weaves a traditional story about raven and coyote. I imagine that he created these stories for his son and daughter, both for fun and by way of explanation. Joy Harjo's story, "The Flood," is a tale which, in years gone by, would have been handed down orally in the Creek Nation and become a traditional tale. The same is true of numerous other stories presented. The late Lorne Simon's story certainly has its place in Native tales but might remind readers of Kafka's "Metamorphosis." Wendy Rose's narrative is, indeed, a poem, but it deals with how language is invented through symbols and thus works into the development of traditional storytelling. We also find something fairly new in Native stories: the political tale such as that written by Drew Hayden Taylor, Phyllis Wolf, and Maria Campbell.

Six of the Native writers included here are from Canada: Maria Campbell, Lorne Simon, Drew Hayden Taylor, Daniel David Moses, Peter Blue Cloud, and the grandmother of all contemporary Native storytellers, E. Pauline Johnson. One, Juan Rulfo, is from below the political border that separates the United States and Mexico.

Here is a hefty pouch of excellent storytelling, a little something for everyone But wait, wait for a cold winter night when temperatures dip to zero or a blizzard is raging. Sit in a circle on the floor with a huge bowl of popcorn and hot herb tea listening to grandmother or grandfather or uncle begin the telling of stories. Neither the Brothers Grimm nor Hans Christian Andersen can out-spin, out-weave, these tellers of tales.

There is a need to acknowledge and thank various people. First, I need to thank all the masterful storytellers who came before and who gathered the people around them in a tipi, hogan, wicki-up, longhouse, mud hut, or whatever habitat to entertain and enlighten those who would carry on these marvels, these great and abiding tales full of wonder, delight, and wisdom. It behooves me to thank the traditional storytellers of today in whatever abode they sit and speak magic, reminding us all of the here and now, of the then and when, here on Mother Earth.

It gives me deep pleasure to thank Elaine LaMattina and Dennis Maloney of White Pine Press for their interest in this project and their interest in furthering Native American culture. Their contribution has been large. Surely I must thank A. LaVonne Ruoff for her contributions to Native Culture, her countless years of hard work and teaching, and for her introduction to this book. Gladly I offer a huge thanks to Andrea Herrera, Jan McVicker, David Lunde, and the students at the State University of New York College at Fredonia, who greeted me with warmth and who shared their own fine, creative works.

Thanks also to Carole Ashkinaze; Neal Burdick; Ellen Rocco of WLSLU-FM; Randy Hill of St. Lawrence University; Chris Shaw, whom I need at my ear constantly; Jeannie Freeman, who kindly chauffered me to so many universities; Mark Nowak for his faith; Ruth Woodward for her patience, her driving, and her valued friendship; Sarah Iselin and Frank Parman for their strength and good humor; Rokwaho for the many stories on the many nights; Ray and John Fadden, who can tell a tale or two; Peg Roy for the bouquets she lavished upon me; Lucy Ferris, a fine novelist of Hamilton College; Mary Davis of the Huntington Free Library in the Bronx; Caroline Hotaling for the terrific car trip to Bisbee, Arizona; Allegra Stewert, who taught me the art of the story; Deborah Ott of Just Buffalo; Aunt Jennie Sanford, who remains an inspiration; Alan Steinberg for his many offerings; Brother Benet Tvedten, who gave and gave; Neal Suprenant and his wife Randy, a former student; Bill Sipze, former student and exciting young poet; my buddies Emily Warner, Lynn Whalen, Eleanor Sweeney, Brett Sanchi, John Radigan, Diane Wager, Anne Burnham, Curt Stagger, Michael and Dee Castro, Jeanette Armstrong; David Fisher for his life's dedication to Native Culture; Karen Faulkenstrom at the University of Arizona Poetry Center; Phil Gallos and Lorraine Wilson, who will write and publish their stories; Anne and Carl Kingsbury of Milwaukee; Caroline Forché, who was an absolute joy to tour America with; my darling niece Martha and her husband, Steve; Kathleen Masterson of the New York State Concil on the Arts; the people at Poets & Writers for helping to keep me on the road all these years; Nancy Moriarty for her bread and chocolate ice cream; Lorie Hosler of Long Lake for her annual writers' night; and, of course, Dean, Michelle, Quino, and my typists, Jen Yarrow and Jamie Kincaid. A tremendous thanks to all the writers and artists whose work is included in this collection, and especially to my fellow-traveler, Eric Gansworth.

—Maurice Kenny
Saranac Lake
The Adirondacks

Introduction

A. LaVonne Brown Ruoff

Stories for a Winter's Night: Short Fiction by Native Americans, edited by Maurice Kenny (Mohawk), captures the imagination and touches the heart. The Native American writers in this anthology vividly illustrate the continuing power of American Indian storytelling. In "The Man Made of Words," N. Scott Momaday (Kiowa/Cherokee) calls storytelling "an act by which man strives to realize his capacity for wonder, meaning, and delight. It is also a process in which man invests and preserves himself in the context of idea." Like the authors in this volume, Native storytellers traditionally told stories both to educate and to entertain their listeners. Through hearing the sacred and non-sacred stories, young Indians learned about—and adults were reminded of—the origins, beliefs, and history of their nations. George Copway (Ojibwe) eloquently describes in *The Traditional History and Characteristic Sketches of the Ojibway Nation* (1850) the importance of storytelling to him and his people: "There is not a lake or mountain that has not connected with it some story of delight or wonder, and nearly every beast and bird is the subject of the story-teller.... Night after night for weeks I have sat and eagerly listened to these stories. The days following, the characters would haunt me at every step, and every moving leaf would seem to be a voice of a spirit." In *Indian Boyhood*, Charles Eastman (Dakota) emphasizes that "very early, the Indian boy assumed the task of transmitting the legends of his ancestors and his race. Almost every evening, a myth, or a true story of some deed done in the past, was narrated by one of the parents or grandparents, while the boy listened with parted lips and glistening eyes." The next evening, the boy was expected to repeat it.

Storytelling remains a strong force in Native American life. When Native people get together, the storytelling begins. Although stories are still told around evening campfires, they are also shared around kitchen tables or at pow wows, conferences, and public storytelling events. Some of my warmest memories are the stories Indian friends told me while we were driving in my van during rush-hour traffic on Chicago's expressways.

Native Americans have continued the storytelling tradition in their fiction. As they mastered English in school, Native American Indians reshaped American and Western European literary genres to fit their experiences and imaginations. Native writers incorporated into these genres the traditions of American Indian oral literatures, tribal histories, and worldviews. Indian writers published their work as early as the late eighteenth century. Because of the importance of educating non-Native audiences about Native American culture and history, American Indian authors, from the nineteenth century through the late 1960s, published more life histories than fiction or poetry. Particularly since 1969, the number of Native American authors writing fiction has greatly expanded as has their audience.

In the early twentieth century, growing numbers of Native Americans began to publish short fiction as well. E. Pauline Johnson (Mohawk), whose story, "The Derelict," is included in this volume, was the first Indian woman to publish collections of short fiction, both of which appeared posthumously in 1913: *The Shagganappi*, stories for boys, and *The Moccasin Maker*, stories about Indian and non-Indian women, plus an essay. D'Arcy McNickle (Salish/Métis), the anthropologist and novelist whose "Train Time" is included here, also wrote short stories, many of which were never published. Birgit Hans collected McNickle's stories in *The Hawk is Hungry and Other Stories* (1992), which was printed many years after the author's death.

Since the late 1960s, Native American authors have increasingly published short stories. For most Native American writers, anthologies have provided essential outlets for their short fiction. One of the earliest of these anthologies was *The Man to Send Rain Clouds* (1974), edited by Kenneth Rosen, which was widely used in Native American literature courses. The measure of how rapidly the field of Native American short fiction has developed since 1974 is that while Rosen's anthology included only six authors, primarily from the Southwest, *Stories for a Winter's Night* includes thirty-five. The past two decades have also seen the publication of short fiction anthologies by American Indian editors, such as Simon Ortiz (Acoma), Paula Gunn Allen (Laguna), and Clifford E. Trafzer (Wyandot). In addition, several collections of regional and tribal Native American short fiction were published in the past decade.

Further, Native American authors have published several short-story collections or editions of their collected works that included short fiction. Authors in this volume whose stories have appeared in such collections include Dwayne Leslie Bowen

(Seneca), Elizabeth Cook Lynn (Dakota), Maurice Kenny (Mohawk), Simon Ortiz (Acoma), Leslie Marmon Silko (Laguna), Luci Tapahonso (Navajo), and Craig Womack (Muscogee-Creek/Cherokee).

White Pine Press celebrates the beginning of a new century of American Indian literature with the publication of *Stories for a Winter's Night*. Maurice Kenny, the editor, is a much-revered mentor and highly respected author. Kenny pioneered in publishing Native American contemporary poetry in his Strawberry Press and *Contact II* journal at a time when Indian poets had great difficulty getting their poetry in print. Throughout his career, Kenny has mentored individual Native writers and championed their work. One of the earliest and strongest voices in contemporary American Indian literature, Kenny is a prolific poet of admirable range. Long noted for his descriptive and lyric poems filled with vivid sensory images, Kenny has achieved great acclaim for books of poetry on Mohawk themes. Three of his books were nominated for Pulitzer Prizes: *Blackrobe: Isaac Jogues* (1982), *Between Two Rivers: Selected Poems,1956-84* (1987) and *Tekonwatonti, Molly Brant, 1735-1795* (1992). *The Mama Poems* (1984), a poignant portrayal of his family, won the American Book Award. In addition to creating poetry, Kenny has also written collections of short fiction and prose, *Rain and Other Fictions* (1990) and *Backward to Forward: Prose Pieces* (1997), both published by White Pine Press.

Kenny's *Stories for a Winter's Night* is an important contribution to the anthologies of American Indian short fiction. The volume introduces the reader to thirty-seven selections by authors representing a variety of Native American nations, primarily those across the United States. Six writers represent Canadian Indian nations, a larger representation from that country than present in earlier, non-Canadian anthologies. In addition, one author comes from a Mexican Indian nation. Kenny grounds the volume in traditional oral literature by opening it with "The Stolen Girl," a story from Cheyenne oral tradition. Although the focus of the volume is on stories by contemporary authors, Kenny pays tribute to the contributions of earlier writers by including Johnson and McNickle (Salish).

The selections in this intriguing collection give readers an introduction to Native American cultures, life experiences, and creativity. Many of the selections reflect the influence of American Indian oral tradition. In "The Bear Hunt," Louis Littlecoon Oliver (Muscogee-Creek) reinterprets in a Salish tale of how one man outwits a bear. Peter Blue Cloud (Mohawk) creates in "Coyote Meets Raven" a delightful, modern trickster story of the rivalry between two Culture Heroes. In "The Flood," Joy Harjo (Muscogee-Creek) recounts the ancient and modern versions of Muscogee stories about the water monster. In "Deer Dance," Evelina Zuni Lucero (Isleta-San Juan), incorporates the myth of the Deer Dancer into her description of the experience of a young girl at a dance. Lorne Simon (Micmac) includes a Micmac spider tale in his "Webs," which is a thoughtful examination of the author's concept of creation and life.

Several writers examine the interconnection between present experience and the supernatural. In "Shapechanger," Inés Hernández-Avila (Nez Perce/Chicano) describes people's fascination with and fear of a mysterious woman. Three selections depict the harrowing experiences of drivers on the road at night: "The Car Wreck" by Dwayne Leslie Bowen (Seneca); "On Old 666" by Carol Yazzi-Shaw (Navajo); and "She Sits on the Bridge," a narrative poem by Luci Tapahonso (Navajo). Some stories portray dramatic experiences that combine the past and present, the real and the mysterious. Anna Lee Walters

(Otoe/Pawnee) describes in "Che" how a young woman's visit to a buffalo jump triggers memories of stories she was told about her people's connection to the buffalo. Elizabeth Cook-Lynn's (Santee/Yankton Sioux) "A Child's Story" vividly depicts a moment of vision and emotion, when a mother is pulled both by her past passion for her child's father and her devotion to her child. In "White-Out," Phyllis Wolf (Assiniboine/Ojibway) creates a searing portrait of a mother tortured by the memories and voices of her dead infants. Gloria Bird (Spokane) examines the mystery of life and the power of destiny in her intriguing "History."

Other selections emphasize the importance of Native American traditional life. Larry Little Bird (Laguna/Santa Domingo) depicts in "The Hunter" the rituals of the deer hunt. John Mohawk (Seneca) emphasizes in "Haksod" the importance of community in his moving portraits of two generations of Seneca elders who transmitted their stories and knowledge to the young. "Tahotahontanekentseratkerontakwenhaki" by Sally Benedict (Mohawk) humorously describes the consequences of being named after a respected elder with a long name. Daniel David-Moses (Delaware) creates a gripping coming-of-age story in "King of the Raft," a moving account of boys' adventures and friendship. Several authors stress the bonds of community and family. In "Hici, Great Aunt Lucy, Oklahoma 1964," Craig Womack (Muscogee-Creek/Cherokee) creates a loving portrait of his aunt, who gently treats the narrator's ailments while telling him traditional and family stories both to soothe his pain and educate his mind. In "Earl Yellow Calf," an excerpt from *Indian Lawyer,* James Welch (Blackfeet/Gros Ventre) poignantly portrays the reactions of an urban lawyer who travels back to his community and family for his grandfather's funeral. Eric Gainsworth (Onondaga) also focuses on community and family ties in his "Benefit Dinner," which depicts how a reluctant, urban son is drawn back to his reservation home by his determined mother. Juan Rulfo's "We're Very Poor" illustrates a family's desperate struggle against poverty and loss of family honor. In "Needles," Ray Fadden (Tehanetorens; Mohawk) expands the concept of family to include pets in this charming description of raising a porcupine.

The relationship between Indians and non-Indians is another theme authors address. Johnson's "The Derelict" describes the moral conflicts an English minister faces in Canada because he has fallen in love with a First Nations woman. McNickle's "Train Time" both vividly portrays the deep love between an Indian boy and his aged grandparents and the wrong-headed determination of an official to send the boy and other Indian children away to school. In "The Panther Waits," Ortiz masterfully combines a realistic scene of drinking buddies talking about the need for a new Native American vision with the retelling of an ancient myth that contains such a vision. "The Blanket" by Maria Campbell (Métis) focuses on conflicts between First Nations people and the Canadian government. Here Campbell also creates a strong portrait of her tough-minded grandmother, who never surrendered. In her striking, narrative poem "Subway Graffiti: An Anthropologist's Impressions," Wendy Rose (Hopi/Miwok) reverses the gaze of the dominant society by analyzing New York subways as archaeological objects as well as by emphasizing the importance of Native American cultural survival. Two authors use satire to make their political points. In her poem, "Nothing to Give," Gail Trembley (Onondaga-Micmac) creates a sharp portrait of a young blonde woman who tries to be a "wannabe Indian," while Drew Hayden Taylor (Ojibway) satirizes in "Oh, Just Call Me an Indian" the controversies over what to call Native people.

Indian humor, so much a part of storytelling and jokes, is well represented in this volume. Some selections are retellings or recreations of traditional stories, such as those by Oliver and Blue Cloud, while others are new tales about Indian life that reflect some of the themes described above. "Peter Schuyler and The Mohican: A Story of Old Albany" by Joseph Bruchac (Abnaki) is a delightful example of political humor, in which, a clever Indian uses passive resistance to outwit Schuyler. Ted Williams's (Tuscarora) "Hogart," excerpted from his novel *The Reservation*, is the rollicking account of a white man who, after moving to the reservation, makes ludicrous and disastrous attempts to become Indian. In "Piegan Still Life," Stephen Graham Jones (Blackfeet) satirizes Indian-Non-Indian relations in his very funny story of how a hapless Blackfeet becomes the object of a manhunt for kidnapping, after a young girl and boy jump into his truck to hitch a ride to their schools.

Several stories focus on community storytelling. Two exemplify the kinds of incidents that become the basis of community stories that tease individuals about their weaknesses and mishaps. "His Wife Had Caught Them Before," Leslie Silko's (Laguna) narrative poem, is a hilarious example of the gossip story. Oliver humorously describes in "The Yellow Cat Incident," how an unmarried, middle-aged woman unwittingly embarrasses herself when she tries to impress male guests. In "Brewing Trouble," Kimberly Blaeser (Chippewa) captures the teasing and bravado of two Indian men as they vent their anger about the release of the first shipment of Crazy Horse Malt Liquor. Robert J. Conley (Cherokee) also depicts community storytelling in his "Dlanusi," in which Cherokee men gather to feast and exchange stories about Dlanusi, their imprisoned, trickster-like friend.

Stories for a Winter's Night offers a rich and varied feast of stories that readers of all ages can enjoy. So, turn off the radio, TV, and computer games. Settle down in a comfortable chair, with popcorn and apple cider at the ready, and let the word magic of the storytellers in this book transport you into the imaginative world of Native America.

References

Copway, George. *Indian Life and Indian History*, 1858. Reprint. New York: AMS, 1978.

Eastman, Charles A. *Indian Boyhood*. New York: Dover, 1971.

Momaday, N. Scott. "A Man Made of Words." In *Literature of the American Indians: Views and Interpretations*. Ed. Abraham Chapman. New York: New American Library, 1975.

The stories
would be braided in my hair
between the plastic comb
and blue wing tips:
...
The stories
have built
a new house.
Oh they make us dance
the old animal dances
that go a winding way
back and back
to the red clouds
of our first
Hopi morning.
...
I feel the stories
rattle under my hand
like sun-dried greasy
gambling bones.

—Wendy Rose
"Story Keeper"
from *The Half-Breed Chronicles & Other Poems.*

THE STOLEN GIRL
TRADITIONAL CHEYENNE TALE
RE-TOLD BY GEORGE BYRD GRINNELL

There was once a young girl who had many men coming to court her. She was the daughter of a chief, and his lodge was pitched in the center of the circle. Many young men came to see her, but she refused them all. She did not care for any of them. She wanted a young man that she could love.

One evening as she sat in the lodge, she perceived a very pleasant smell in the air, and wondered what it came from. She wanted to look out and see, but did not wish to go to the door and herself be seen; so she took her mother's awl and pierced a hole in the lodge skins and, peeping through the hole, she saw a young man standing not far off.

When she had looked at him for a little while, she liked him, and determined that she would go out to see who it was. She did so, and as she walked past him he spoke to her, and she stopped. Then they talked to each other, and the girl asked him who he was, and why he had come; for she saw that he was a stranger. The young man said: "The home of my people is far from here, and I have come to get you. Come with me, and we will go to my father's lodge."

The young man spoke pleasantly, and the girl, after she had thought a little while, said to him: "Very good, I will go with you. Other young men want me, but I do not want them. I will go only with you. First, however, you must let me go back and get my awl and sinew and my quills." The girl went into the lodge and made up a bundle of her things, and then came out again and said to the young man: "Now, I am ready. Which way do you live from here? In which direction must we go?"

"I live toward the rising sun," said the young man. "There are many camps of my people there." They set out toward the east.

As they were going along, she said to him: "What is your name? What do they call out when you ask your friends to come to a feast with you?"

"My name," he said, "is Red Eye."

They traveled along for some time, and it was almost night when they came near to the camp. There were many trees where the camp was pitched, and all among the trees you could see the light shining through the lodge skins. They passed into the circle of the camp, and went up to a big lodge standing in the center, and when they got to the door, the young man and the girl stopped. Through the lodge skins they could see the shadows of many men sitting about the fire, and could hear them talking and laughing. The young man's father was speaking. He said to the others: "My son has gone far away. He has gone to get a chief's daughter to marry. He has seen her and liked her, and now he has gone to get her. After a time, if he has good luck, he will return with her." So the old man talked about his son.

At last Red Eye said to the girl, "Come, let us go in." He first went into the lodge. When his father saw him he was surprised.

He said to him: "Why, my son, I did not think to see you again so soon. I hope you have had good luck."

The girl followed the young man into the lodge, and went over and sat on the women's side. She saw her father-in-law speaking to her husband, and she noticed that he had a very sharp nose; and after a time, as she looked about, she saw that all the men sitting around the lodge had sharp noses. The lodge was nicely fixed up, and the linings handsomely painted. On the beds were many nice warm buffalo robes.

At the girl's home there was great trouble. The chief's daughter had disappeared, and no one knew what had become of her. Her father and mother were crying because their daughter was lost. All the young men were out searching for her. They could not find her, nor any trace of her. When they could not find her, her father felt still worse, and said to the young men who were searching for her, "The young man who finds my daughter shall marry her."

When the girl awoke in the morning, she found that she was in a big hollow tree, and all about the tree were sitting mountain rats. The buffalo robes on which they had been lying were grass nests.

A young Cheyenne man was out looking for this girl, and as he passed a great hollow tree the girl came crawling out from it.

"Girl," he said, "where have you been? Everyone in camp is in great sorrow because you are lost. We have been searching for you everywhere."

"Friend," said the girl, "the rats stole me away, and brought me here to this tree." Then the young man took her back to her father's lodge, and afterward he married her.

That was the beginning of rats stealing things from people.

THE FLOOD

JOY HARJO

It had been years since I'd seen the watermonster, the snake who lived at the bottom of the lake, but that didn't mean he'd disappeared in the age of reason, a mystery that never happened. For in the muggy lake was the girl I could have been at sixteen, wrested from the torment of exaggerated fools, one version anyway, though the story at the surface would say car accident, or drowning while drinking, all of it eventually accidental.

But there are no accidents. This story is not an accident, nor is the existence of the watersnake in the memory of the people as they carried the burden of the myth from Alabama to Oklahoma. Each reluctant step pounded memory into the broken heart, and no one will ever forget it.

When I walk the stairway of water into the abyss, I return as the wife of the watermonster in a blanket of time decorated with swatches of cloth and feathers from our favorite clothes. The stories of the battles of the watersnake are forever ongoing, and those stories soaked into my blood since infancy like deer gravy, so how could I resist the watersnake, who appeared as the most handsome man in the tribe, or any band whose visits I'd been witness to since childhood.

This had been going on for centuries; the first time in my memory I carried my baby sister on my back as I went down to get water. She laughed at a woodpecker flitting like a small sun above us, and before I could deter the symbol, we were in it. My body was already on fire with the explosion of womanhood, as if I were flint, hot stone, and when he stepped out of the water he was the first myth I had ever seen uncovered. I had surprised him in a human moment. I looked aside but I could not discount what I had seen.

My baby sister's cry pinched reality, the woodpecker a warning of a disjuncture in the brimming sky, and then a man who was not a man but a myth. What I had seen there were no words for, except in the sacred language of the most holy recounting, so when I ran back to the village, drenched in salt, how could I explain the water jar left empty by the river to my mother who deciphered my burning lips as shame?

My imagination had swallowed me like a mica sky, but I had seen the watermonster in the light of lightning storms, breaking trees, stirring up killing winds, and had lost my favorite brother to a spear of the sacred flame so certainly I would know my beloved if he were hidden in the blushing skin of the suddenly vulnerable. I was taken with a fever and nothing cured it until I dreamed my fiery body dipped in the river where it fed into the lake. My father carried me as if I were newborn, as if he were presenting me once more to the world, and when he dipped me I was quenched, pronounced healed. My parents immediately made plans to marry me to an important man who was years older but would provide me with everything I needed to survive in this world, a world I could no longer perceive, since I had been blinded with a ring of water when I was most in need of drink by a snake who was not a snake, and how did he know my absolute secrets, those created at the brink of acquired language?

When I disappeared, it was in a storm that destroyed the houses of my relatives; my baby sister was found sucking on the hand in the crook of an oak. And though it may have appeared otherwise, I did not go willingly. That night I had seen my face in the sacred fire, strung on the shell belt of ancestors, and I was standing next to a man who could not look me in the eye. The oldest woman in the tribe wanted to remember me as a symbol in the story of the girl who disobeyed, who gave into her desires before marriage and was destroyed by the monster disguised as the seductive warrior. Others saw the car I was driving as it drove into the lake early one morning, the time the carriers of tradition wake up, before the sun or the approach of woodpeckers, and they found the emptied six-pack on the sandy shores of the lake. The power of the victim is a power that will always be reckoned with, one way or the other.

When the proverbial sixteen-year-old woman walked down to the edge of the lake to call out to her ephemeral destiny, within her were all sixteen-year-old women from time immemorial, and it wasn't that she decided to marry the watersnake, but there were no words describing the imprint of images larger than the language she'd received from her mother's mouth, her father's admonishments. Her imagination was larger than the small frame house at the north edge of town, with the broken cars surrounding it like a necklace of futility, larger than the town itself leaning into the lake. Nothing could stop it, just as no one could stop the bearing down thunderheads as they gather for war overhead in the war of opposites.

Years later when she walked out of the lake and headed for town, no one recognized her or themselves in the drench of fire and rain. The children were always getting ready for bed, but never asleep, and the watersnake was a story that no one told anymore. She entered a drought that no one recognized as drought, the convenience store a signal of temporary amnesia. I had gone out to get bread, eggs, and the newspaper before breakfast and hurried the cashier for my change as the crazy woman walked in, for I could not see myself as I had abandoned her some twenty years ago in a blue windbreaker at the edge of the man-made lake as everyone dove naked and drunk off the sheer cliff as if we had nothing to live for—not then or ever. It was beginning to rain in Oklahoma, the rain that would flood the world.

WHITE-OUT

PHYLLIS WOLF

In the penny postcard she sent home, she was pictured standing in a white high-collared waist. Twenty-five buttons could be
counted down the front. The rest were lost in a voluminous
skirt that skimmed her ankles.

    —Do you remember this?

    —No.

    —This was taken when you were at school.

    —Was it?

    —Do you remember knitting dishrags?

    —Oh, hell. I do. That's all we ever did was knit
dishrags That's why I don't like to knit. Go to school to knit
dishrags.

She looked out the window and saw something no one else
could see. She held her stomach delicately as young women hold
theirs when it is first filled with life, smoothing hands over
rounded curves. Her stomach wasn't gently rounded but pro-

truded sharply to one side, yet she smoothed it with her hands. She held the contorted stomach as she stood to move toward the window. It was heavy and pulled at the intestines. The pain had made her cheeks hollow and she stood bent, waiting.

—Do you want to go outside?

—It's cold out.

There were only a few inches of snow on the ground but clouds the same color of snow had come. In the distance, she could not see where the earth ended and the sky began. Her hands moved over the stomach gently and caught it up from underneath. She thought of the babies, the bastard babies she buried. Her daughter was looking through a box of old letters.

—Who's this you're with?

—I don't remember.

—You're not even looking.

She turned toward the picture her daughter held up. It was a man in an ill-fitting suit two sizes too small. His hair was split down the center and greased flat to his head. His ears stood out.

—I don't remember.

She turned toward the window. She could hear cries being muffled. Infant cries muffled by dirt. She stood in front of the, window and wiped her hands against her dress. Her stomach pulled. She looked down at it. Her cheeks had become even more hollow. No, she didn't remember and what she did she didn't want to remember. Small mouths filled with hard dirt. And the days would be like this where the sky was indistinguishable from the earth that she would pour dirt into those mouths. The mouths would be open and they would cry, but the crying would stop after a while. She only heard the cries now when her stomach pulled at intestines and then she would have to cradle the stomach in her hands to make the crying stop. She cradled the stomach now but cries still came from out-side the window. Infant cries that pierced the stomach where she stood looking out to swirling white clouds that rose up from earth.

NEEDLES

TEHANETORENS/RAY FADDEN

There was a little Indian boy at Akwesasne. His name was Joe Brown. He lived on Racquette Road. One day Joe come to school with a little porcupine, just a baby. He still had quills even though he was very small. I said Joe, you should never take a little animal away from its mother. That animal's mother loves that little porcupine just as much as your mother cares for you. That's a cruel thing you did taking that baby away from its mother. He said, "Mr. Fadden, I didn't take it away. I was in the woods, Fulton's woods, and he was on the log. And I looked all around for the mother and he must have been lost, so I took it home." Well, I said, I realize now that you didn't mean to do this, but now I've told you; whenever you find a little raccoon or porcupine in the woods, any baby animal, just leave him alone. The mother knows where he or she is. The mother will take a little porcupine, put him on a stump, and tell him not to move, stay right there. Then she goes off in the woods, she eats leaves and bark, and forages around. She can tell by the way her breast feels when it's time to feed the little one. She makes a noise. The little one, it has good ears. They come together, he eats his dinner, he follows the mother. I said, how long ago did you pick that little fellow up? "A day and a half ago." Ahh, I said, it's too late. She's already come, and she thinks somebody killed her baby. She's probably crying inside. I said, it's too bad but we'll have to bring it up right here in school. We have to give him a name. So, what do you suppose we call him? Needles. Because he had a lot of little needles.

Even though he was a baby porcupine, he wasn't afraid of us. He figured we were his mother. He was so small he couldn't get a bottle nipple in his mouth. We had to feed him with an eye-dropper. We warmed the milk, put a little sugar in, and then you fed him. The only trouble is, he eats every three hours, all night long. I used to take him home with me. He stayed under the kitchen sink. When I first brought him home I let him sleep right on the bed. Well, ten o'clock at night he starts calling. Just like a little kid calling for something to eat. What are you going to do? I warmed the milk and I'd feed him. Then he'd go back to sleep again. Three hours later, all over again. Three hours later, all over again. I was glad when he started to eat out of a dish. And him and my dog got along okay. They got along fine.

When Needles was a little baby, and he did his business on the floor, it wasn't too bad. He was just a baby, but when he got to weigh thirty pounds, and he did it on floor, phew, what a smell. You know that stuff that you wash things with? Ammonia they call it, it makes your eyes smart. So my wife said, "You're going to teach him to do that on paper or he's going out." So just like training a dog, every time he did it, I'd pick him up like a cat, put his nose in it, and then put him on the paper. Believe or not, I taught him to do it on the paper. Then

I'd burn the paper. But I didn't get downwind from it.

He knew how to open the cupboard door and he slept under the kitchen sink. When he got full grown, I taught him how to open the back door. I figured he was getting big enough to be on his own. So I'd let him loose and follow him. You know how slow a porcupine is, he didn't know I was following him. He always headed for the hill behind my house because there was a female porcupine up there. I don't know how he knew, but there was one up there.

One day Needles stood in front of the kitchen door, and he was going back and forth. I told my wife, this is cruel. I said, we could treat him and give him all the food in the world, but he wants to be free. I said, an eagle, he may be starving up in the sky, but he would rather starve to death than to be put in a hen coop and be made a chicken out of him. Let's let him go and pray he doesn't walk up to some human being, and pray he doesn't get hit by a car. So this one time, I didn't follow him. I opened the back door and he waddled down the steps, and he disappeared into the woods.

My wife and I, we couldn't sleep. He was like our kid, you know. We loved him. I went walking up and down the road with my flashlight thinking he might come down the road. My wife told me to sleep out on the porch. I said he can open the door. She answered, "Sleep out on the porch!" She's the boss. I sleep out on the porch. During the night, I heard gnawing. You know, if you put salt on a stump, the porcupines chew the stump and leave your house alone. I placed the light over there, looked at the porcupine; I looked close, but it wasn't Needles. Three other porcupines came during the night. No Needles. Meanwhile, no sleep.

It was just getting light in the east, when I looked down the trail, and there came Needles just as fast as his fat legs could carry him. I said "Needles!" with happiness in my voice. He just glanced at me, rushed right by me, rushed to the steps, rushed up the steps, rushed across the porch, rushed to the door, opened the door with a slam, and rushed to the paper. He held it all night in the woods. It's a true story. I put paper all the way across the kitchen floor and he took it all before he was through.

Well, they always said you should start a talk with a funny story. There you have it, except it is all true.

Coyote Meets Raven

Peter Blue Cloud

Coyote was visiting in British Columbia. "Hey," he asked, "do you people have guys like me around? Who's your local joker and doctor anyway?"

A Raven flew down and perched on Coyote's shoulder to croak out, "I am the greatest doctor there is or ever was! I am my own beginning and my own ending. Mine was the first voice ever!"

Coyote looked at the big black bird and said, "You sound just like the missionaries down to the south, but I'll take you at your word, and you can get off my shoulder now. You're kind of heavy, you know?"

"Too late! Too late! I've got your power in my belly now. You never again be what you used to be!'"

"As long as you don't start yelling, 'Nevermore! Nevermore!' it's all okay with me," Coyote responded, studying the Raven and making plans. "Well," he said, "you're in your own country and have an advantage, but let's anyway have a power contest, okay? But let's do it friendly and play a handgame since I see that your people up here play the same gambling games we do down south."

And so they gambled for two days and a night. On the second night coyote began growing bored and decided to leave his body and travel around. He left his gambling concentration in a hollow hallucination of empty skin and took off.

He walked down to the beach to be with the ocean. There at thd beach's edge stood a huge totem pole. Atop the pole was a great bird like none other Coyote had ever seen. There was something about the bird which drew him and he climbed up there for a closer look.

The Thunderbird was a sleeping power, a force awaiting its own time. It was transfixed in dreaming. Coyote sat way up there on a wing thinking of Raven and studying Thunderbird.

Well, he thought, as long as I am Coyote I might as well leave a trick behind me. Yes, I think I will sing Raven into this bird and leave him captured here. He's a good gambler, I'll have to admit, but I get the feeling that he thinks he's better than I am.

Coyote closed his eyes and began humming. His humming became words:

> Ho, ho, guts and blood,
> heh, heh, dreaming power.
> Raven, I call you.
> Raven, I sing you.
> Fly here to this place.
> Be captured here forever.
> Ho, ho, heh, heh, ho!

He was just beginning the third round of the four-round song when he heard a croaking laugh. He opened his eyes to the interruption. He no longer sat atop the Thunderbird; the Thunderbird sat upon him, its claws dug into his skull.

Only the beak of the Thunderbird moved when it spoke, still made of cedar and clattering. "Hah, you guessed it, I see. Yes, it is me, Raven. You have captured nothing but yourself for I am not to be captured." Then Raven continued his own song to lock Coyote into the totem.

And Coyote finished his power-capture song.

"Look down to the beach, Coyote. Don't you see a dozen of me down there feasting and talking?"

"Eating rotten fish and squawking, yes! But you are also captured in this pole. And look over there at that spruce tree up the hill. See that grey movement? That's Coyote!"

There was a roar from Thunderbird for that great creature had come to life. Its voice was that of howling winds and crashing waves.

"You miserable wretches! You pitiful, puny self-lovers! You punk lice living in the armpits of yourselves! How dare you disturb my meditation! Don't you know that I can end time by waking? No, of course you don't! And you probably don't even know that I helped create you! A mistake, I now see.

"I am going to make two lesser totems and put you side by side on them. I'm going to put each of you atop one, looking at the ocean and unable to see the other. Then you can argue into eternity.

"Perhaps you'll even learn to meditate and begin to know the beauty of Creation. And further, I'm going to make each of you little bit like you might be someone else, maybe Eagle or Wolf. "I will let you taste real beauty and power while keeping your puny egos intact.

"Coyote, when a part of you returns to the desert country,

you'll find Raven and his nation waiting for you. And every time you hunt you will leave part of the feast for Raven. And Raven will thank you with the croaks and graws you find so discordant. Perhaps each of you will learn to live with and respect the other. Now go!"

And Thunderbird once again became a cedar meditation. And Raven and Coyote studied the ocean for many seasons, each sitting atop his own totem pole.

Coyote woke up in a dry wash north of Gallup. The cries of ravens had awoken him. "Coyote, Coyote, wake up, we are hungry! Wake up, Coyote!"

"I'm lean and I'm mean," said Coyote to no one in particular. He drank at a spring, then washed his face. He sat on a small hill to watch the sun rise. A raven perched close by and let out a tentative croak. Coyote opened his backpack and took out a can of pork and beans and a couple rounds of somewhat dried-out frybread. As he ate he threw some of the food to the raven.

They didn't speak to one another but grimaced each time their eyes met, giving looks which just might pass for smiles.

And we might add that to this very day...etc. But, we won't

Dlanusi

Robert J. Conley

Gog'ski, or Smoker, was having a big feed at Rocky Ford in the Goingsnake District of the Cherokee Nation. Rocky Ford was not a place anyone would recognize while passing through, but it was a place the Cherokees who lived there recognized as a community. The homes of the residents of Rocky Ford were scattered throughout the hills, and even when two or three families might be located within easy walking distance or even within shouting distance, they were still not within view of each other. A near neighbor's home was always obscured from sight by the thick growth of trees, the winding roads and the ups and downs of the Ozark foothills. What made Rocky Ford a community was purely and simply the sense of community of its inhabitants. They attended the same church, a Cherokee language Baptist church, and they got together frequently for community gatherings. They also knew and minded each other's business as if it were their own.

Anyway, Gog'ski was having a big feed at his home. Perhaps

there was an occasion for this feed, perhaps not. That information has been obscured by the passing of a century and perhaps a decade. Hogs had been slaughtered, much food had been prepared, and a large and jovial crowd had gathered around Gog'ski's log cabin. The crowd consisted mostly of full-blood Cherokees, and the conversation was all in the Cherokee language. Gog'ski was running around acting busy, playing the host, but he finally slowed down a bit to catch his breath, stopping in a small cluster of men who had been engaged in idle chatter.

"This is a good gathering," said Walkingstick to Gog'ski.

"Everyone should get plenty to eat," said Gog'ski. "There's lots of food. I killed three hogs."

"That might not be enough if Dlanusi was here," said Yudi, and his comment was answered by a round of good-natured laughter.

"Yeah," said Gog'ski, "old Leech could really put away the hog meat. Well, I guess he still can."

"He could if he could get to it," said Walkingstick. "I bet that's the worst part of jail for Dlanusi. They don't feed them much hog meat in there, I bet. Ask Shell."

"More like hog slop," said Shell, or Uyasga.

"Say," said Yudi. "You were over there in that Fort Smith jail with Leech, weren't you?"

"Uh huh," said Shell. "For too long."

"At least they let you out," said Gog'ski. "They won't ever let Dlanusi out. Not until they hang him, I guess."

"When will they do that?" asked Yudi.

"I'm not sure," said Gog'ski, wrinkling his brow as if in deep thought. There was a pause, and then Shell spoke again.

"Today," he said.

Everyone looked at him.

"They're supposed to do it today," he said.

The awkward silence continued until Gog'ski stood up and paced nervously.

"Today," he repeated. "I guess we shouldn't be here having such a good time. Not if they're going to hang Leech today. He could be hanging right now."

Yudi shivered, and Walkingstick looked at the ground. Gog'ski's right hand went instinctively to his own throat. He looked at Shell.

"You've only been home about a week," he said. "You were in the same cell with Dlanusi, weren't you?"

"Yes, I was," said Shell.

"Did he know then when it would be his last day?"

"Yes. He knew."

"How was he?" said Gog'ski.

"What do you mean?"

"Well," said Gog'ski, "was he sad? Was he afraid?"

"No" said Shell. "He was cheerful. He joked. He seemed happier than I, even though I knew I was getting out."

Everyone was quiet then, listening to hear what more Shell might have to say. The group had gotten a little larger since the discussion of Dlanusi, the Leech, had begun.

"It was maybe seven days before I got out," said Shell. "Sgili equa, the Big Witch, came to visit Dlanusi, and he brought some soap, the kind we make at home. There was never enough soap in the stinking jail, and the guards let Dlanusi keep it. After that, he washed every day, maybe two, three times a day. He was so clean.

"The day before they let me out, Dlanusi dipped his hands in the water bucket, and he was holding his soap. Then he stood up, and he started rubbing the soap, and he lay back on his cot. He was making a lot of bubbles, and pretty soon the bubbles started to rise up and float, and Dlanusi started to laugh, a happy sounding laugh. The bubbles were floating up and going out the window between the bars and just floating away. Dlanusi stopped laughing, but he still had a big smile on his face, and he said to me, 'You see that?' He was watching the bubbles float out the window between the bars. 'You see that?' he said. 'I can get out of here just that easy.' then I looked closer, and inside each bubble I could see a tiny little man sitting and smiling at me as his bubble rose up slowly and floated out the window, between the bars and away, carrying him with it. That's what I saw while I was there in jail with Dlanusi."

Shell stopped talking, and the others just sat there as if stunned. At last Gog'ski got up and clapped his hands together. "Well," he said, "does anyone want to go over there and toss some marbles with me?"

The group broke up, some following Gog'ski to play marbles, the old Cherokee game of marbles, more closely resembling lawn bowling than what white men call marbles, some others wandering until they found someone else to talk to, perhaps to repeat the strange story Shell had just told them. Shell stayed right where he had been all along. He just sat there. Later the women called out that the food was ready, and the men all lined up to be served. They were just sitting down when a horseman came riding toward the house. All watched to see who was coming, and when he got close enough to recognize, Shell was the first one to speak.

"Dlanusi," he said.

Dlanusi rode right up close. He was sitting on a shiny saddle on the back of a big, black stallion that pranced and snorted, and he was dressed flashy, like a cowboy, in black leather boots and a black vest over a clean white shirt. His long black hair folded on his shoulders, and he wore a black, flat-brimmed hat on his head. His broad grin showed his white teeth flashing out of his dark face.

"Hey," he said, in a loud and cheerful voice, "did you leave me anything to eat here?"

Deer Dance

Evelina Zuni Lucero

Trini had been told not to come because nothing good ever happened at the bar.

Now here she was dancing with Reynard with his cool, distant air, and the half-moon curve of his smile. She remembered the Deer Man. Trini smiled when she caught herself looking at Reynard's feet. His shiny leather boots were as fancy as the rest of him. Reynard's shirt, a crisp, black-and-white checkered print, had thunderbirds cross-stitched on the front yokes and was neatly tucked into his bluejeans. A large silver buckle sat atop his firm belly, threading a tooled leather belt which blazed REYNARD on the back. He was like a buck, sleek and full, well muscled, surefooted; his neck was smooth and graceful, his skin an even bronze-tone. He possessed an easy smile that flashed like a lightning bolt, illuminating his face and sparking movement behind his photogreys.

Yes, he was good-looking enough to fit the story that Auntie

Rosa liked to spook them with as children:

The tall, handsome stranger strode into a wedding dance, com-
manding attention with his silent entrance, looking neither to the left
nor right. No one knew who he was though he looked vaguely familiar, like someone's cousin's cousin. The bride's family thought he must
be the guest of the groom's family, and the groom's family assumed
he was known by the bride's side. He carried himself with grace and
sureness, head erect, meeting all questioning eyes and answering them
with careful indifference. Large turquoise stones, conspicuously old
and heavy, dangled from his earlobes. His long hair was pulled back
in an old-time style. He leaned against the wall, smoking a cigarette,
a glint of amusement in his dark, slanted eyes.

All the young, single women and even the restless married ones
watched, ready to catch his eye, hoping to be the one he'd ask to
dance. After a long time—the dance was almost over—he asked the
prettiest, most popular girl to dance. The other women sighed and pretended they didn't care, but they watched enviously out of the corner
of their eyes. They saw how he tenderly gazed into the depths of her
eyes, and how he spun her across the room in movements as smooth
as silk against silk.

The girl forgot who she came with, forgot that her sweetheart might
have meant something to her, that he stood in the corner sulking. A
woman letting her hair down, she danced on with the stranger. The
songs became soft sighs, each dance a yearning. As the last song was
ending, screams and shouts filled the air. The band stopped. The
crowd parted. The young girl who was dancing with the handsome
stranger lay lifeless on the floor.

In the confusion of the moment, the stranger almost slipped away,
but he was stopped at the door by belligerent, red-eyed young men.
Once again, terrified screams paralyzed the crowd. In the sudden
hush that came upon the room, someone cried out, "Look! Look at

his feet! He has the feet of a deer!" The stranger smiled, brazen and fearless. He pushed his way to the door unchallenged and walked out. Later, his deer tracks were found beneath all the windows of the hall.

Rosalee heard the story while she was at the Indian School from the matrons who insisted that it was true. During the deer-hunting season, Rosalee and other women would joke, saying, "Now that the men are gone, let's go on a hunt of our own for a two-legged dear." It took a while before Trini caught the pun. She used to wonder why they would want to look for the Deer Man and risk being danced to death.

Only in a place like this could that happen.

Reynard smiled at her.

She looked away.

NOTHING TO GIVE

GAIL TREMBLEY

The woman was young, blond, beautiful
like the girls in slick magazines who model
jeans. She chose to wear a bone choker
with an ermine tail as though it is possible
to appropriate a culture by wearing its artifacts.
She read a poem in which she said that she was
the white girl who always wanted to be Indian
when she grew up. I sat feeling sick, recognizing
 that strange phantom pain in the gut, listening
to her romantic distortions about Eagle Boy dancing
in her dreams, about cruel Indian men who undressed
her and then scolded her for being naked before
them when she was on her moon. She invented
unreality because she refused to witness the real
hard work of living in a world distorted by forced
assimilation, by faked authenticity, by loss
that beat in counter rhythm near the heart
and made the whole world seem out of balance.
She did not speak of struggle, stolen land,
the Earth raped so that strangers could reap
great profits no matter what the cost. Her desire
was for vision to fill an empty life. One more
taker, she invented ceremonies that mystified,
that made healing seem a hollow exercise untied
from the web of light that weaves things seamlessly
into being, untied from the people who for generations

shared a sense of what made things whole in a given
place. I sat and watched speechless, caught,
too paralyzed to walk away and make a scene,
aware how often revelation is impossible to explain.

THE HUNTER

LARRY LITTLEBIRD

Maybe it was because I was a child and saw it that way, or maybe it really is the way I remember it, growing up in my mother's village.

It is fall. There is a special clarity in the way light appears at this time of year. And it gives my memory a sense of another time, a time when my young eyes can see beyond the haze and the world stands out, still, brilliant, and defined. In the fall, all talk and thoughts turn to hunting. As the stories of the deer and the hunter unfold detail by detail, in my child's mind, images of the deer appear and take shape.

They say the deer is a spirit. A creature of God's creation, it needs supplication, understanding, and reverence. It is a blessing, a gift bestowed upon humankind as a remembrance of our own life's interconnected course, an interwoven thread from the beginning of all living time. It is meat for the body and soul. Endowed with a keen sense of sight, smell, and hearing plus additional uncanny abilities beyond human dimension, this creature cannot be simply slaughtered and used. The deer's realm is the pristine spaces of mountain and plain, its very domain is a santuary. Its essence is life; to kill it is to waste it.

This new and wondrous creature begins to occupy me, looming magnificently magnified and imagined in my thoughts as I roam mesas and arroyos playing, as I eat and sleep.

I want to be a hunter, one of the men afield in the fall, gun in hand, bandolier of shiny bullets around my waist, a bright red kerchief about my head. Can I be a man who will endure the rigors of the hunt? The all-night prayer and singing? A man who from daylight till sunset, without food, without drink, will evidence the stamina of a strong people? I wonder.

With a child's anticipation and delight, the fall evenings are spent around the little outdoor fires on the village edge waiting into the night for the signal that will tell everyone a hunter returns. For seeming nights on end. We wait until at last the bright orange spark that lights the shadow of the far southern hill sends me scurrying with the other boys and girls toward the only road by which the hunters will enter. Gathering excitedly at the road's edge, laughing and whispering, speculating about which party of men are returning, our noisy exuberance is suddenly cut silent. A low murmuring sounds from the far deep night. The joyous rise of men's voices singing their songs of the deer coming home to our village reaches us through the darkness.

Someday I will arrive home like these men, my face painted to signify my sacred purpose, greeted reverently by the people, blessed and made welcome. I dream of that day, but how?

One day my grandmother simply tells me, "Day by day, little by little, you will learn. Keep your eyes open, your mouth shut and become obedient to those in authority around you. Life is sacred to us, and you are sacred. You carry it in your heart the best you can. Treat all things as you want to be treated, then some day you will be ready." It is simple and I believe her. But I still want to kill a deer.

With a little boy's forgetfulness, these questions I ponder so seriously easily give way to other equally important concerns as the season passes. Will there be enough snow this year for my homemade sled I've worked so hard to find enough scrap boards to make? Will I ever learn to spin my brightly painted wooden top, whipping off the tight string as accurately as my older cousin? Will my small frail hand ever grasp the correct grip on the beautiful glass marble that would allow me to win a few? The seasons come and go, visibly blending one into another, and even though I still leave more marbles in the ring than fill my pockets, visions of the deer never quite leave me.

During this time I learn to use a home-made inner tube band slingshot until cans, bottles, even objects tossed into the air are accurately and consistently knocked down. After that, proficiency with a rifle comes easily. Even then, something tells me hunting is more than expertise with a weapon. Gradually, I am obsessed by one recurrent thought, "to kill a deer without wasting it."

The year of my first deer hunt, my uncles carefully instruct me on what a man does when he wants to hunt. I do as I am taught; I do it all correctly but I don't kill a deer.

"Killing a deer isn't everything to hunting," my uncles say. "Fasting and praying, a man works hard giving his self to the spirit the deer belongs to. We are only human, we cannot say what our giving should bring. Yes, we want badly to bring home that big buck; we can only work truthfully at doing that. The Creator will see our honesty; we must believe our reward will come about. There should be no disappointment."

Trying not to feel disappointed, I think all this over. I prepared so carefully—my rifle, my bullets, my actions, my thoughts, my prayers. Where am I at fault? Then I remember.

I remember that little boy sitting by the outdoor fires watching for the returning hunters. I remember what he felt in his heart when he saw the stripe-painted faces of the men arriving home from the deer's mountain sanctuary, their beings permeated with invisible blessings, strength, well-being.

I remember water that is made holy as the paint is washed from their faces by the women. I remember the little boy who is told to drink that sacred water. I remember eagerly drinking that murky brown liquid, the taste of sweet sediment in my mouth. The grownups laugh and make joking remarks but I drink it anyway because I believe them when they tell me it will make me a strong hunter. I feel my body shudder as the essence touches my young heart that wants only to be a hunter.

It is the desire to be a hunter who will not waste a deer's life that I remember. My feet have touched the mountains where deer live; I have breathed in the same air and drunk of their water. I've gotten close, yet no deer has come to my hungry gun. There is no fault. Had I killed a deer that first year, would I have recalled the little boy who wanted to be a hunter? Or remembered the child who believed the stories old men and old women tell in that other long ago time?

Surely, the deer is a spirit, and I must die if I am to be one. Day by day, little by little, as I embrace and struggle with this gift, my worldly desires must die, my physical needs must die. I must die to the selfish lusts that would entice my body and entrap my soul, until at last, unthinking and clear-eyed, innocent like a child, I am free to believe and know the secret pulsing in the hot flowing blood the hunter hunts. And, somewhere, the red living waters of the pure-eyed deer wait for me.

Subway Graffiti:
An Anthropologist's Impressions

Wendy Rose

New York City, 1978

1.
Day-glo signs of survival
in impossible places
 the City
and we primates
consider our position
with full-armed pitches
through the holes
in our future.
We have not been here long enough
to know if there's a reason
to mate. We may be extinct now
as we tunnel through rock,
crush cockroaches
whose record is stronger
and longer than ours.
> Words on subway walls were cries of help
> arrangements made
> treaties abandoned
> death threats
> turned into rumbles
> with name and number
> recorded.

Art starts
pragmatic
becomes design
    dies
    unseen.

2.
My California-born senses
feel the subway
as an earthquake
strangely regular;
I grip the seat
and wait to see
if I should stand
in a doorway or duck
under a table.
    Reality is changed
    from three thousand miles.
    About this earthquake writing:
    fifty feet into island rock
    the people rumbled
    into each other,
dueling for power.
The slippery cliff walls
tell of war, of prayer,
of hunts long over
into the night, of idleness,
of romance, of dripping water,
of scurrying rats, of fires
generating on the ties
and dying, of logical regular
metal-slick strokes

returning through evolution \
to basics.
>I can't read most of it.
>Style is now design
>and the messages remain
>secret, hieroglyph
>not hieratic.

Manhattan has no Rosetta Stone
in the earth to be found
and deciphered
by my probing
colonial tongue.
Train by train,
station by station,
they are
an underground blur.

3.
$$$$ Hunger, engraved shells
>that will feed the deer
>who shelter in my belly.
>I will give you the ocean currents
>if you will salt my rotting meat.
>I will kill the rabbit for you
>if you will make it warm my feet.
>I worship what I kill
>I worship what I eat
>I worship what it means
F— M.A.E. A blow for mankind
>upon womankind.
>From the bruises on your flesh

you will give me a son.
With the hand that wrestles
a digging stick to earth
you will grasp and I will dig
all the deeper with my seed.
The weak are to be run over
by my rod of power;
always we must know who is stronger
by the broken bones of my women
and my boys.

DUKES RULE!   Our leaders
eat themselves bare.
They will not plant,
they will not hunt.
They are wasteful
yet they sharpen their tongues
on my labor. Not they
but something greater
keeps peace in the village
or lets it go.
These ones trade wives for manioc.
macaw feathers for turquoise;
their power is bound to flesh
and they are always
always hungry.

STRIKE!   Obsidian breaks
under elk antler.
Flakes, fingernail-shaped,
spin to my feet.
This is shaping,
this is ruling, this is eating,
this is organizing, this is symmetry

this is god, this is copulating
this is real, this is to be defined,
this is beyond description.
We will defy
what we need
and we will be the shapers.

SCORE   Our language is precious.
These signs mark our clans
as we are dried
from where we emerged
to this place chosen for us.
We speak, we watch, we sing for signs.
We torment, we tease,
we will not let you hear the words
for they are sacred.
This is who we are;
we are the words.
You may someday hurt
with the parts left behind,
words that were left
vibrating on the ground,
parings of hair, toenail,
spirit and song.

THE CAR WRECK

DWAYNE LESLIE BOWEN

One time there was a bad car wreck and three men were killed. It was a real bad one.

Sometime later there was a carload of men coming back from drinking in the next town. The only guy awake was the driver because all the others were asleep or passed out. Then one of the tires went flat and he had to stop. He stopped in the very same place where the car wreck had happened. The driver got out to look at the flat tire and then he tried to wake up the others so they could help change the tire. But nobody wanted to get out or they just turned over and went back to sleep. The driver got mad at them but he knew that they wouldn't get out. So he started to change the tire by himself. Because he was drunk it took him a long time to get the car jacked up. He didn't have the jack set right either. Just as he got the wheel off the car, the jack slipped and the car crashed down on the ground. The bumper was laying on the ground and the jack couldn't be replaced under the bumper. By now the guy was really mad and he tried to wake up somebody again but they just kept snoring away. He tried once more to get the jack back under the car but he couldn't. So he just gave up and leaned against the car and took a big drink from his jug. Just then somebody walked up and stood in front of the car This person asked if he could help out. The driver answered that he wanted help. The person said that he had two more friends with him and that they would help out if they could have something to drink. The driver said that he had enough for everybody. But the driver began to feel funny because he couldn't see the faces of these men who were going to help him. The headlights were shining toward the ground and he could only see their legs. Their shoes looked all dried up and cracked The three men grabbed the car by the bumper and picked it up off the ground. They held it up until the driver was able to put the spare on. Then they let it back down. The driver turned around to say something to them but they had moved to the other side of the car out of the light. He asked if they wanted a drink now and they said that they did. So he opened the door to get out another jug. When he opened the door the inside light came on and he turned around to give them the jug. When he saw them in the light, he lost his breath and fell to the ground. He could not move because he was so scared by what he saw.

All three men were dead men. They all had skull heads and they were destroyed. One had the top of his head scraped away. They moved forward and the man tried to scream. They took the jug and each one took a good long drink. They put the jug down and they moved away back into the darkness. The man on the ground tried to yell and tried to get up but he couldn't. Just then his brother looked out the window and saw him laying on the ground. He got out of the car and went over to help his brother off the ground. The driver told his brother what just happened. Then they went and woke up the rest of the men in the car. They told them what just happened too. They all got scared. So they poured out some whiskey onto the ground and said some words to the ghosts which were just there. Then they all got back into the car and left there in a hurry

Hogart

Ted Williams

One year Chesta Raagit geh brought a white man onto the
reservation to live with him among the pines. His name was
Hogart. Not like his brother, Manylips, Chesta was fairly quiet
in his relationship to the chiefs and churchy Indians of the reservation. Nobody questioned Chesta's way of making a living
because he took odd construction jobs here and there, even
when he was way past retirement age; he never had no birth cer-
tificate. Chesta also made lots of friends with people off the
reservation, and for some reason, many Syrians. His big house
was in a big grove of huge pine trees and every weekend was
party weekend within the pines. Under the counter of picnic
and party foodstuffs passed a fairly steady stream of moonshine
or white lightning. Here's probably where Hogart came in.
Maybe he knew the recipe for white lightning.

Indians like music. Only thing wrong was, unless they were
drunk, the beat of the music had to be perfect or the Indians

---

couldn't stand it. Being as there was a strong temperance society on the reservation, the biggest share of Indians didn't drink anything stronger than pop. Or if they did, they snuck it—from places like Chesta Raagit's Geh. Hogart had a fiddle which he played good enough to make nickles from at the drunken Syrian parties. He was yet to learn that his playing wasn't good enough for sober Indians; even some drunk ones.

Gradually, Hogart got to meeting other Indians besides Chesta. He got to liking them. In fact after a while he even began copying them. He grew to like the way they lived. Before he knew it, he began trying to BECOME an Indian.

How he found out that his fiddle playing wasn't quite good enough, he first got to be friends with an Indian named Clay-born. Clay-born played mouth organ, guitar, and bass drum all at the same time; or sang instead of mouth organing. Clay-born married my goo-sood (my mother's aunt) and she had a son named Char. Clay-born and Char used to play for me sometimes when I had a birthday. Char sang and played guitar. Clay-born was the boss and got to know Hogart through the parties in the pines. He also got to know the juice that flowed under the picnic benches. Clay-born, then, got Hogart to fiddle while the white lightning burned. Hogart, though, couldn't cut the mustard at any sober parties because he couldn't follow the perfect beat that Clay-born's fat leg laid down on the bass drum.

If Hogart failed to be Indian as a musician, he would at least LOOK like an Indian. He took his shirt off and came out of the pines to get a good tan on his skin. This move failed too, though, because all he did was burn and peel, burn and peel.

Next he tried to speak the Tuscarora language. Before too long, he made a big mistake. He liked this Indian woman named Bird. He tried to learn the Indian word for "bird" but instead he called her by a word which, although it is very close to bird, means a woman's private place. A good slap in the mouth sealed his Tuscarora word learning lips right then and there.

The closest Hogart came to being Indian while he was alive was, he became very poor. In order to stay alive, and being white, the thing he thought of was to go into business. He became a shoe and clothing salesman. What with the Indians sewing a lot of their own things and buying the rest at Dig-Dig's (secondhand stores like the Salvation Army stores and Goodwills) Hogart went broke. This puzzled Hogart because the Indians, in general, looked fairly fat while he was starving into a skeleton.

At first, he got pretty discouraged because lots of Indians planted corn and squash and stuff and he knew he wasn't cut out for hoeing, being as he was afraid of a sunstroke. Some Indians, though, didn't plant. Some sewed beadwork. Old women mostly. Hogart had big fingers and couldn't find a thimble to fit 'em and he quit trying beadwork because he kept getting jabbed by both ends of the needle.

The next thing he discovered on the reservation, though, did wonders for him. He discovered welfare. On the day his welfare check came you could expect to see Hogart on his way to Sanborn, pushing a wheelbarrow for groceries. This seemed to be a step in the right direction and probably he should have left well enough alone right then and there. That is, he should have quit while he was ahead, but no; Hogart wasn't satisfied.

All this struggling to be Indian was too much for his nervous system and his hair turned white as snow. All the tricks he used to dye it only made the Indians laugh so he gave up on hair color, even though white hair was a big setback.

Next he decided he might hunt with the Indians. Somebody on the reservation reminded him that a hunter needed a gun and exchanged a .22 rifle for one welfare check. The rifle turned out to have a hair trigger on it. Hogart no more than put a bullet in it when he forgot and set the butt of the gun on the floor. Bam! The bullet hit the ceiling and a good-sized piece of plaster came down and clunked Hogart's head. Also, on the way to the ceiling, the bullet cut the skin on Hogart's belly and mangled one of his ears. Of course it had to be the ear that Hogart used to rest against the fiddle when he played it. Worse yet, Chesta Raagit yelled at him for shooting in the house. Well—so much for Hogart's hunting experience.

The first time Hogart left the pine grove with the mangled ear, some Indian saw it and said, "You were about one inch from hell." This got Hogart to thinking. At the end of his thinking he decided that he better hurry up and join the church. He chose the Baptist church because it had a bigger membership and this way he figured he'd be more "in" with more Indians. The baptism was in February, right after revivals and when he saw the hole chopped through the ice he began changing his mind. It was too late. Oonook was too strong for him and forceled him to Thraangkie, the minister. A struggle took place but Hogart lost. Some say he wasn't properly baptized because in the struggle, some parts of him managed to stay out of the icy water. I saw the baptism and if Hogart could do anything, he could cough up a storm. I think he breathed in some water though, but just the same, he coughed until his face looked almost Indian color.

When communion Sunday came, Hogart was right there, waiting for his bread and grape juice. As he waited, he looked around. Here was lots of Indians fast asleep. So he went to sleep, too. Suddenly someone jabbed him awake. Here was the plate of bread in front of him. "Thank you," he said, popping one of the little squares into his mouth and swallowing it. His face turned bright red as he realized that he was supposed to wait for the signal.

Finally, Hogart ran out of ideas on how to be Indian. Jeeks came to his rescue. Jeeks told Hogart that he needed to eat genuine Indian food. Hogart agreed and got invited to eat at Jeeks'. It was night when he got there. He had been invited to a supper of Nekhrehh soup. These are little brown tree frogs that have a dark brown streak trailing off their eyes to down their little backs. They are great jumpers during the day, even climbing rough barked trees. They hang out in big wet woods. How Jeeks' mother caught them, she would take a lantern at night and put it near the edge of a spread-out blanket. Then she would do with her tongue almost like a police whistle and tree frogs would come jumping from all over—into the blanket to see the light. Well, when she got back to hungry Hogart that night and when he saw her dump all these little Nekhrehh squirmin' and pissin' into her soup kettle of boiling water, he suddenly had to use the outhouse. He excused himself to go out but he never came back in to eat his Indian food.

When he got back to Chesta Geh (means Chesta's place) he told Chesta that he had given up trying to be Indian. "Once white, always white," he moaned.

Chesta took one look at Hogart and says, "No wonder! Look at yourself!" Hogart tried to roll his eyes inward to look at himself. Chesta says, "Go wan down to Dig-Dig's and get you some Indian duds."

When he got to Dig-Dig's he became confused. However, he did learn why the Indians call such places Dig-Dig's. Many people were digging into the secondhand clothing, trying to find whatever was at the bottom of the piles before somebody else got there. Hogart got bumped and pushed and ousted out of the scramble until he ended up with the leavings. Still, Chesta had probably unknowingly given him the secret that would solve all the tryings-to be-Indian that Hogart had messed up on without coming to Chesta in the first place. So he began picturing in his mind, just how Indians DO dress. He pictured Old Holland stomping through the winter weather with a long summer overcoat flapping unbuttoned behind him. Winter was coming but if Holland could do it, so could Hogart. So that's what he bought. A summer long coat with no buttons.

The next item of news on the reservation was that Hogart was dead. Pneumonia.

I give Hogart boo-coo credit for trying. But you know what? Even dead, Hogart failed. Instead of burying him on the reservation, the poorhouse stuck him in the ground someplace near Cambria.

KING OF THE RAFT

DANIEL DAVID MOSES

There was a raft in the river that year, put there, anchored with an anvil, just below a bend, by the one of the fathers who worked away in Buffalo, who could spend only every other weekend, if that, at home. The one of the mothers whose husband worked the land and came in from the fields for every meal muttered as she set the table that that raft was the only way the father who worked in the city was able to pretend he cared about his sons. Her husband, also one of the fathers, who had once when young gone across the border to work and then, unhappy there, returned, could not answer, soaking the dust of soil from his hands.

Most of the sons used the raft that was there just that one summer in the usually slow-moving water during the long evenings after supper, after the days of the fieldwork of haying and then combining were done. A few of them, the ones whose fathers and mothers practiced Christianity, also used it in the afternoons on sunny Sundays after the sitting through church and family luncheons. And the one of the sons who had only a father who came and went following the work—that son appeared whenever his rare duties or lonely freedom became too much for him.

The sons would come to the raft in Indian file along a footpath the half-mile from the road and change their overalls or jeans or swimsuits among the goldenrod and milkweed on the bank, quickly, to preserve modesty and their blood from the mosquitoes, the only females around. Then one of the sons would run down the clay slope and stumble in with splashing and a cry of shock or joy for the water's current temperature. The other sons would follow, and, by the time they all climbed out onto the raft out in the stream, through laughter would become boys again.

The boys used that raft in the murky green water to catch the sun or their breaths on or to dive from where they tried to touch the mud bottom. One of the younger ones also used to stand looking across the current to the other side, trying to see through that field of corn there, the last bit of land that belonged to the reserve. Beyond it the highway ran, a border patrolled by a few cars flashing chrome in the sun or headlights through the evening blue like messages from the city. Every one of the boys used the raft several times that summer to get across the river and back, the accomplishment proof of their new masculinity. And once the younger one, who spent time looking at that other land, crossed and climbed up the bank there and explored the shadows between the rows of corn, the leaves like dry tongues along his naked arms as he came to the field's far edge where the asphalt of that highway stood empty.

Toward the cool end of the evenings, any boy left out on the raft in the lapping black water would be too far from shore to hear the conversations. They went on against a background noise of the fire the boys always built against the river's grey mist and mosquito lust, that they sometimes built for roasting corn, hot dogs, marshmallows. The conversations went on along with or over games of chess. Years later, one of the older boys, watching his own son play the game with a friend in silence, wondered if perhaps that was why their conversations that year of the raft about cars, guitars, and girls—especially each other's sisters—about school and beer, always ended up in stalemate or check. Most of the boys ended up winning only their own solitariness from the conversations by the river. But the one who had only a father never even learned the rules of play. One sunny Sunday after church, late in the summer, the one who had only a father already sat on the raft in the river as the rest of the boys undressed. He smiled at the boy who had gone across through the corn, who made it into the water first. Then he stood up and the raft made waves as gentle as those in his blue-black hair

"I'm the king of the raft," he yelled, challenging the boy who had seen the highway to win that wet, wooden square. And a battle was joined, and the day was wet and fair, until the king of the raft, to show his strength to the rest of the boys still on shore, took a hank of the highway boy's straight hair in hand and held the highway boy underwater till the highway boy saw blue fire and almost drowned. The story went around among the mothers and the fathers, and soon that son who had only a father found himself unwelcome. Other stories came around, rumors about his getting into fights or failing grades or how his father's latest girlfriend had dyed her Indian hair blonde. And the boy who almost had drowned found he both feared the king of the raft and missed the waves in his blue-black hair.

One muggy evening when pale thunderheads growled in

from the west, the boy who had almost drowned, who had the farthest to go to get home, left the raft and the rest by the river early. On the dark road he met the king, who had something to say. They hid together with a case of beer in a cool culvert under the road. The king of the raft was going away with his father to live in Buffalo in the United States and thought the boy who had almost drowned could use what was left of this beer the king's father would never miss. The boy who had almost drowned sipped from his bottle of sour beer and heard the rain beginning to hiss at the end of the culvert. He crawled and looked out in time to see the blue fire of lightning hit a tree. In the flash he saw again the waves in the king's blue-black hair, the grin that offered another beer. The boy who had almost drowned felt he was going down again, and, muttering some excuse, ran out into the rain. The king yelled after him that old insult boys use about your mother wanting you home.

The boy who had almost drowned found he could cross through the rain, anchored by his old running shoes to the ground, though the water came down like another river, cold and clear and wide as the horizon. He made it home and stood on the porch, waiting for the other side of the storm, hearing hail hitting the roof and water through the eaves filling up the cistern. Later, out of the storm, he could still hear far-off a gurgling in the gully and a quiet roar as the distant river tore between its banks. The storm still growled somewhere beyond the eastern horizon.

The raft was gone the next evening when the boys came to the bank, and the current was still too cold and quick to swim in. No one crossed the river for the rest of the summer. The king of the raft never appeared again anywhere. In the fall, a rumor came around about his going to work in the city and in the winter another one claimed he had died. The boy who had crossed through the rain thought about going down even quicker in winter river water. Then a newspaper confirmed the death. In a traffic accident, the rain boy read. None of the boys had even met that impaired driver, that one of the fathers, surviving and charged without a licence. One of the mothers muttered as she set another mother's hair about people not able to care even about their kids. The rain boy let the king of the raft sink into the river, washing him away in his mind and decided he would someday cross over and follow the highway through that land and find the city.

SHAPECHANGER

INÉS HERNÁNDEZ-AVILA

Would you let me tell you of a woman who found her way when the sun met the dusk and the power of the sands kept her by the sea as only she could do? She walked into the waters, hands outstretched. She greeted the waves and sang to herself as the sun watched over her. She bathed herself and left her grief. She breathed new life into herself and felt the sun touch her heart and face.

She was a shapechanger. With her hands she could fuse the edges of nearness, bring worlds close to shimmer in her eyes. Laughter was her companion and moved easily with her in the dance of love.

Some people called her *bruja* because they could not otherwise explain her. Even some Coyotes feared her, feared the swooping into their very insides this bird could do, soft-spoken creature lighting in each corner to set their souls on fire, just by being herself.

On one of her *peregrinaciones* to Old Mexico, one man saw her and within moments swore his love to her, swore by the cross of Chalma, swore even as he completed a *penitencia*, his knees still aching. He stood up in the church and forgot his vows, his promises, his wife, his life, and wanted to be hers.

She laughed, and in the face of everyone, in the space of ceremony, she took that time for her own. She savored the meeting like he'd been sent from outer space to signal her of other times to come, because, for a while, she had been alone.

She intended to be free that time. The other women shuddered in trepidation, growing smaller by the instant to disguise their prisons of cowardice and learned submission. Some yearned for her daring, yearned to call the day and night their own, to walk and talk and be as they pleased. They longed to laugh with abandon, to joy as she did, to speak what their *conciencias* told them should be said, as she did. When they could, in secret, they would search her out for comfort, and sometimes they left their old lives, gathering strength within themselves from day to day, finding courage in their inspiration of self-invention, becoming shapechangers themselves.

Others hated her and wanted to kill her, to erase her face from the face of the world. Some had longed to bang her head into stone, hoping the force would disintegrate the face and the face would be no more. They refused to grant her what they would not grant themselves. A studied vehemence had found a home in them and he had no intention of leaving, having won his hosts over with terror clothed in what he called traditional garb, convincing them that their intended way of life was to succumb. As their life force was drained, he became revitalized.

She had come to recognize more quickly the ones who would not see her, so sometimes in her shapechanging she became a hummingbird, or a pregnant, bursting cloud, or a song, or a soft light at dawn, to cajole these ones who lived in fear out of their hidden places and into the circle of life for them to be healed. And as she danced her dance, smiling and holding her head high, she cared for herself as she had never done in the other days, before she learned to shapechange.

bruja: witch
peregrinaciones: pilgrimages
penitencia: penance
Chalma: a place of pilgrimage (south of Mexico City) within the Conchero
       dance tradition of Mexico
conciencias: consciences/consciousnesses

Brewing Trouble

Kimberly M. Blaeser

The day G. Heileman Brewing Company releases the first shipment of Crazy Horse Malt Liquor, Grey Jay Bunker sits on a bench, hunched over, reading the bottle. Suddenly, he straightens up, stuffs it back in the paper sack, winds the top of the sack tight around the neck of the bottle, and sinks it deep into the side pocket of his overcoat. Then he sits squinting into the space in front of him.

A mountain begins to materialize out of the near distance, no a man, a big mountain of a man—hell, it's Luke Skywalker. Grey Jay knows he must be in another dimension. This doesn't frighten him because he believes it possible, it has happened before. What worries him most is the timing. He had been looking at the odd buckskin-clad figure in a headdress on the bottle, wondering if it was supposed to be a frontiersman or an Indian. Hell, he had been expecting Crazy Horse, not Luke Skywalker. How do you talk to some cult movie figure?

"Hey, Bandit. Snap out of it, man. Jeez, Bunker, you look like some kind of crazy pigeon bum, hanging out on a park bench, wearing that godawful army-reject coat. We been looking for you. Want to go to kareoke tonight at Front Row?"

Grey Jay's head snaps back toward his right. "Huh?" It takes him a few seconds to register his friend's presence. Then, like a man who has drawn fire, he turns quickly again to scan the park in front of him. Finding it empty now, he releases his breath in a barely audible "Damn."

"Bunker...kareoke?"

Still distracted, Grey Jay takes up the conversation. "Hell, Craig, you can't sing. Margaret can't drink. And I feel like fighting every time I get close to pastels or designer labels. What's the point man?"

"Free food."

"Listen, Craig, you see anyone when you were coming over?"

"I told you, Margaret..."

"No, I mean someone here with me?"

"Why? Who you been with?" He parks himself beside Grey Jay, stretching his too-long legs straight out in front of him.

"Never mind. You seen this yet?" Grey Jay pulls the bottle out of his pocket and hands it to Craig. Craig unwraps it and lets out a long whistle. They sit in silence while Craig reads the label to himself: "The Black Hills of Dakota, steeped in the history of the American West, home of Proud Indian Nations. A land where imagination conjures up images of blue-clad Pony Soldiers and magnificent Native American Warriors..." Grey Jay sees Luke Skywalker peek out from behind a tree then duck back. He looks quickly to see if Craig is still there. He is.

"Jesus. Listen to this crap: 'A land where wailful winds whisper of Sitting Bull, Crazy Horse and Custer. A land of character, of bravery, of tradition. A land that truly speaks of the spirit that is America.' I just don't get it. What does the murder of a religious hero have to do with beer?"

"TV. "

"What?"

"It has to do with TV and movies and the NFL and the American League and Babe Ruth candy bars and Tammy Faye Bakker..." Grey Jay spots Luke Skywalker again who waves and then begins a mocking game of peek-a-boo.

"Yeah, well I say let's start our own little pub brewery, no, no a winery." Craig holds the bottle by its neck as he gestures with it for effect. "We'll call our first wine 'Washington's Cherry Blush' and we'll work our way along until we get to the the top of the line, the two-hundred-dollar-a-bottle stuff and we'll call that 'Grapes of Wrath' or the 'Last Supper Wine.'" As a series of odd expressions play across Grey Jay's face, Craig stops talking to watch. It reminds him of his old hunting dog, Animosh, who would growl and bark at the thin air. He gives Bunker an elbow nudge. "Hey, you listening to me. This is good stuff I'm spouting, Bandit."

Grey Jay pulls his attention back to Craig and gives him a little snorting laugh. "I gotcha."

"Well maybe. But I'm wasting my talent on you." Worried now, Craig puts on a hearty voice. "Come on you old Camp Robber you, let's go find Margaret." The two begin walking along the park's cobblestone path.

"You remember Star Wars?"

"Uh huh."

"I was wondering, was that Skywalker character a good guy or a bad guy?"

"Hell, Bunker, I have enough trouble trying to remember if I'm a good guy or a bad guy. Come to think of it I don't know that I ever had it figured out to begin with. I mean about me, not Skywalker. So what's with Star Wars? You wanna rent it?"

"No, I saw the guy that's all."

"Well, yeah, we all saw him a couple of years ago."

"No, I mean I saw him for real—today."

Craig's voice fills with pleading and warning. "Bandit..."

"Yeah, and I ain't even opened the damn bottle. What do you think it means?"

Craig kicks at a few tall blades of grass that line the edge of the pathway. "You know you are weird man. Dammit, Bandit, everyone else that has visions sees something that at least seems spiritual. But you, you see grey jays, common camp robbers, bandit birds hauling off crazy stuff like books and babies. Now you're seeing movie characters. Other people see Elvis, who at least was alive once, but you see someone else's imaginary character and someone from outerspace to boot."

The two men have stopped next to an oak. As Grey Jay smiles broadly at his friend he says, "Can't afford to be picky these days." Then, despite his bulky coat, he grabs hold of the lowest branch, swings his legs up, and easily pulls himself upright onto the branch and begins reconnaissance of the park.

Craig continues his tirade, pacing about the base of the tree, kicking the air now, and yelling up at the other man. "And you don't fuckin' know for certain that you are related to that medicine man from Canada. You know even your Aunt said it ain't for certain. Besides which you got some common genes in you, too. Why the hell don't you use those for a change." He waits for a response from Grey Jay. None comes, and he continues. "I mean it man. It's clear as shit something's brewing, but you ain't roping me into no more crazy business. No protests, you hear? No sneaking around like some Indian Greenpeace disrupting anybody's business. I care just as much as you about social justice and all, but I got a life to lead. I got a woman and a baby on the way and all that civil disobedience crap is just gonna land us in jail again."

Craig looks up to see how his friend is taking everything. Grey Jay is perched in the tree as comfortably as his namesake might be, lying on the branch on his back with one leg dangling over the side. As if in resignation Craig hands up the bottle. Grey Jay pockets it again, sits up, and reaches down to help pull his friend into the tree. The two sit in silence watching the park world below.

Finally Craig takes the bottle and begins turning it in his hands again. "You know, Bandit, after all these years, no one knows where Crazy Horse was buried."

"They do now." Grey Jay waits for his buddy to look up before he adds, "Because they've buried him." He holds the stare-down a beat or two before he grins. "Another shipment's coming in tomorrow. You remember the Boston Tea Party?"

"But that was about taxes, man. I don't think it's really the right angle. Listen, it says here in bold letters PRODUCT OF AMERICA. We could sure as hell get a lot of mileage off of that in a press release, if we were going to do this, which we ain't. What the hell you grinning at Crazy Bird?"

BENEFIT DINNER

ERIC GANSWORTH

Eyes following a dark-necked, ponytail-wearing guy out at the doughnut shop/convenience store, where he conveniently showed up, maybe saving me from the longest walk of the nineties, I hung up the phone where my mother explained that she had to cook dinner for my brother, forty-six, because his wife left him last year for the new good fortune of tax-free cigarettes and gasoline. Over the pay phone lines, I could hear her clanking in her old, worn kitchen as she prepared his supper and told me I'd just have to wait. Because he deserves more than even one additional disappointment after a hard life's work, every night, his roast beef or whatever, is on the table, his laundry and ironing are done, his floor is vacuumed, and his kitchen is spotless—though that last is not too hard to accomplish, as he never cooks.

He's always at her house for dinner, except on Saturday nights, when he takes one of a series of new women, non-smoking and non-driving, to nice restaurants. "As it all should be," my mother says on the thankful free nights she is abandoned. "Don't a hard-working Indian man deserve those things, and don't you know it's five-o-five, when he always arrives?" she continued, just before I hung up, as I argued in the hundred degree doughnut shop that I thought he could manage dinner on his own, just this once. "And it's *your* bad fortune, she emphasizes, "that your old Mustang died on the intersection of Military and Buffalo and you don't have a ride home. What are you doing, living in the city, anyway? You're just going to have to wait until I have the table set, 'cause if you still lived out here, you wouldn't have this problem. There'd be plenty of people to give you rides....You know, if you got a ride out here, it would be much easier," she rattled, as if I hadn't thought of this, and before she could come up with anymore, I took her advice the moment I saw that old Jay stroll in, and as he bought two jelly doughnuts and a coffee, his name came to me, the only break of the day.

When I asked him if he could take me home, he said sure. "Want one?" he asked, offering me one of his doughnuts as we got in the truck. "I'm not supposed to have them," he tells me, "but I'm going to that benefit dinner tonight—and damn! if it don't start until eight o'clock. Who eats dinner at eight, anyways? It's for Patrick, you know, who got caught in that plant explosion?" he elaborated, discussing the accident my cousin's husband had been involved in, which had landed him long months of reconstruction in Intensive Care. It had been a fluke, the reaction of some randomly misplaced chemicals mixing with others. The dinner proceeds and good wishes were to go toward defraying costs. Patrick was overwhelmed with the support and uncomfortable at all the attention he was receiving, not wanting to inconvenience anymore with this dinner, but everyone knew he would handle himself with grace and style, because that's just the kind of person he is. "Is that where you're going?" Jay asked.

I had to confess that I didn't even know they were having a dinner for him, the flyers not reaching as far as my mailbox, and when Jay headed us in the direction of the reservation, I could not tell him that I meant my place in the city when I asked him if he'd take me home. As I climbed from the truck at my mother's house, he told me I had some traces of white on my face, so I brushed the powdered sugar from my cheeks and the pale flakes, caught on small breezes, headed back toward the city. Starting my shuffle through the familiar crushed stones of my mother's driveway, I could see my brother's car, blocking hers at the end, as if her world stopped until he decided his needs were met, and actually, this was probably true. I could smell the roast beef, even from the road, and I knew she always had enough for an unexpected son returning home. By the time I stepped in the door, my plate had magically appeared on the table and ice settled in my glass, because that, after all, is what she has trained herself to believe a hard working Indian man deserves.

PETER SCHUYLER AND THE MOHICAN: A STORY OF OLD ALBANY

JOSEPH BRUCHAC

When Peter Schuyler was the Mayor of Albany, he used to walk along the busy docks on the wide Hudson River where ships sailed in and out each day. One day, on his customary walk, he saw a Mohican man sitting with his feet dangling over the edge of one of the piers, watching the ships and the river and quite obviously doing nothing useful. Mayor Schuyler was a man much devoted to doing useful work. So he approached the Indian and said, "You there, why don't you do some work, you lazy good-for-nothing?"

"Why don't you work, Mayor?" said the Mohican.

"What?" said Schuyler. "I work all the time. I just do it within my head."

"Ah-huh," said the Mohican, "I begin to understand. You just give me some work to do and then I will do it."

"Good!" said Schuyler, "You can go to my barn and kill the calf there for me. We have been intending to eat that calf and there is a man who wants the skin."

"I agree," said the Indian. "First, though, you must pay me. It is a long walk to your barn."

Though Schuyler thought all Indians were lazy, he knew that they could be trusted to keep their word. So he handed over a shilling in advance and the Indian left. In a bit more than a hour, he came back to the place where Schuyler still stood, watching the ships.

"Well," said Schuyler, "where is the skin?"

"You only asked me to kill the calf," said the Mohican. "If you wanted me to skin it, you should have asked me. Give me another shilling and I will skin it and dress it out for you."

Reluctantly, the Mayor pulled out another coin and the Mohican set out for the farm. An hour later he came back with the skin and handed it to the Mayor. But as he gave it to him, he said. "Those dogs there on your farm look as if they want to eat that calf."

"What?" said Schuyler. "Did you not hang it up where they couldn't reach it?"

"Hang it up?" said the Indian. "You only asked me to skin it and dress it out. Give me another shilling and I will run back and hang it. But you must do so quickly. Those dogs looked hungry."

By now, Mayor Schuyler was getting angry. He reached into his pocket and found he had only a two-shilling piece. "Here," he said, shoving the coin at the Indian, "give me back a shilling in change."

The Mohican man did so and then trotted off, Schuyler's coins jingling in his pouch. While he was gone, Mayor Schuyler thought over all that had just happened. There was no way he

STORIES FOR A WINTER'S NIGHT

would let an Indian get the better of him. The Mayor decided he would teach this Mohican a lesson he would not forget. Taking out a piece of paper, he wrote on it, *The bearer of this is a rogue. Give him a good beating.* Then he signed it, folded it and sealed it.

When the Mohican returned an hour later, Schuyler smiled. "Would you like to earn another shilling, my friend?" he said.

"Certainly, my friend," said the Indian, holding out his hand for the coin.

"Good," said the Mayor, "This note must be delivered to the Captain up at the fort. I want you to see that it is delivered into his hands. He will give you something special for doing this. Then I want you to come back to this same spot and when you see me again you can tell me what you think about things."

The Mohican took the note and started on his way. However, though he could not read, he did not go far before he began to think about things, indeed. The smile on the Mayor's face as he left him had been much too broad. As the Mohican walked along, he saw coming his way one of Schuyler's English servants, a young man with a reputation for disliking Indians. The Mohican walked up to him and held the paper so that the young Englishman could see the Mayor's seal on it.

"Do you see this?" the Mohican said. "The Mayor wants this note delivered to the Captain at the fort. The person who delivers this note will be given something special, but I am not certain how to take it to the Captain."

"Why are all you Indians so stupid?" said the young Englishman, grabbing the sealed note out of the Mohican's hand. "I shall see that it gets to the Captain." Then the young Englishman headed for the fort, eager to get what was coming to him.

The Mohican man followed at a prudent distance. When he

saw the Captain read the note and then ordered his men to take hold of the young Englishman and beat him, the Mohican turned around and went back to the wharf.

Later that same day, when Mayor Schuyler came looking for him, he found the Mohican back in his familiar spot, watching the ships go by and dangling his feet in the water.

"You ignorant savage," said the Mayor, "I thought I told you to take that paper to the Captain."

"You said the note was to be delivered into his hands. I saw that it was delivered. Then, having done so, I came back here as you asked."

"Hmph," said the Mayor. "Perhaps you think you made four shillings, but you did not. That second shilling I gave you was made of lead. It is worthless."

"I know," said the Mohican man, "that is why I gave it back to you in change for the two-shilling piece."

"You rascal," said Mayor Schuyler, "How is it that you manage to get by with such impertinence?"

"Ahh," said the Mohican, smiling as he watched the ships on the river, "I do it within my head."

WE'RE VERY POOR

JUAN RULFO

Everything is going from bad to worse here. Last week my Aunt Jacinta died, and on Saturday, when we'd already buried her and we started getting over the sadness it began raining like never before. That made my father mad, because the whole rye harvest was stacked out in the open, drying in the sun. And the cloudburst came all of a sudden in great waves of water, without giving us time to get in even a handful; all we could do at our house was stay huddled together under the roof, watching how the cold water falling from the sky ruined that yellow rye so recently harvested.

And only yesterday, when my sister Tacha just turned twelve, we found out that the cow my father had given her for her birth-day had been swept away by the river.

The river started rising three nights ago, about dawn. I was asleep, but the noise the river was making woke me up right away and made me jump out of bed and grab my blanket, as if the roof of our house were falling in. But then I went back to sleep, because I recognized the sound of the river, and that sound went on and on the same until I fell asleep again.

When I got up, the morning was full of black clouds and it looked like it had been raining without letup. The noise the river made kept getting closer and louder. You could smell it, like you smell a fire, the rotting smell of backwater.

When I went out to take a look, the river had already gone over its banks. It was slowly rising along the main street and was rushing into the house of that woman called La Tambora. You could hear the gurgling of the water when it entered her yard and when it poured out the door in big streams. La Tambora rushed in and out through what was already a part of the river, shooing her hens out into the street so they'd hide some place where the current couldn't reach them.

On the other side, where the bend is, the river must've carried off—who knows when—the tamarind tree in my Aunt Jacinta's yard, because now you can't see any tamarind. It was the only one in the village, and that's the reason why people realize this flood we're having is the biggest one that's gone down the river in many years.

My sister and I went back in the afternoon to look at that mountain of water that kept getting thicker and darker and was now way above where the bridge should be. We stood there for hours and hours without getting tired, just looking at it. Then we climbed up the ravine, because we wanted to hear what people were saying, for down below, by the river, there's a rumbling noise, and you just see lots of mouths opening and shutting like they wanted to say something, but you don't hear anything. That's why we climbed up the ravine, where other people are watching the river and telling each other about the damage it's done. That's where we found out the river had carried off La

Serpentina, the cow that belonged to my sister Tacha because my father gave it to her on her birthday, and it had one white ear and one red ear and very pretty eyes.

I still don't understand why La Serpentina got it into her head to cross the river when she knew it wasn't the same river she was used to every day. La Serpentina was never so flighty. What probably happened is she must've been asleep to have let herself get drowned like that. Lots of times I had to wake her up when I opened the corral gate for her, because if I hadn't she would've stayed there all day long with her eyes shut, real quiet and sighing, like you hear cows sighing when they're asleep.

What must've happened then was that she went to sleep. Maybe she woke up when she felt the heavy water hit her flanks. Maybe then she got scared and tried to turn back; but when she started back she probably got confused and got a cramp in that water, black and hard as sliding earth. Maybe she bellowed for help. Only God knows how she bellowed.

I asked a man who saw the river wash her away if he hadn't seen the calf that was with her. But the man said he didn't know whether he'd seen it. He only said that a spotted cow passed by with her legs in the air very near where he was standing and then she turned over and he didn't see her horns or her legs or any sign of her again. Lots of tree trunks with their roots and everything were floating down the river and he was very busy fishing out firewood, so he couldn't be sure whether they were animals or trunks going by.

That's why we don't know whether the calf is alive, or if it went down the river with its mother. If it did, may God watch over then both.

What we're upset about in my house is what may happen any day, now that my sister Tacha is left without anything. My father went to a lot of trouble to get hold of La Serpentina when she was a heifer to give to my sister, so she would have a little capital and not become a bad woman like my two older sisters did. My father says they went bad because we were poor in my house and they were very wild. From the time they were little girls they were sassy and difficult. And as soon as they grew up they started going out with the worst kind of men, who taught them bad things. They learned fast and they soon caught on to the whistles calling them late at night. Later on they even went out during the daytime. They kept going down to the river for water and sometimes, when you'd least expect it, there they'd be out in the yard, rolling around on the ground, all naked, and each one with a man on top of her.

Then my father ran them both off. At first he put up with them as long as he could, but later on he couldn't take it any more and he threw them out into the street. They went to Ayutla and I don't know where else; but they're bad women.

That's why father is so upset now about Tacha—because he doesn't want her to go the way of her two sisters. He realized how poor she is with the loss of her cow, seeing that she has nothing left to count on while she's growing up so as to marry a good man who will always love her. And that's going to be hard now. When she had the cow it was a different story, for somebody would've had the courage to marry her, just to get that fine cow.

Our only hope left is that the calf is still alive. I hope to God it didn't try to cross the river behind its mother. Because if it did, then my sister Tacha is just one step from becoming a bad woman. And Mamma doesn't want her to.

My mother can't understand why God has punished her so giving her daughters like that, when in her family, from Grandma on down, there have never been bad people. They were all raised in the fear of God and were very obedient and were never disrespectful to anybody. That's the way they all were. Who knows where those two daughters of hers got that bad example. She can't remember. She goes over and over all her memories and she can't see clearly where she went wrong or why she had one daughter after another with the same bad ways. She can't remember any such example. And every time she thinks about them she cries and says, "May God look after the two of them."

But my father says there's nothing to be done about them now. The one in danger is the one still at home, Tacha, who is shooting up like a rod and whose breasts are beginning to fill out, promising to be like her sisters'—high and pointed, the kind that bounce about and attract attention.

"Yes," he says, "they'll catch the eye of anyone who sees them. And she'll end up going bad; mark my words, she'll end up bad."

That's why my father is so upset.

And Tacha cries when she realizes her cow won't come back because the river killed her. She's here at my side in her pink dress, looking at the river from the ravine, and she can't stop crying. Streams of dirty water run down her face as if the river had gotten inside her.

I put my arms around her trying to comfort her, but she doesn't understand. She cries even more. A noise comes out of her mouth like the river makes near its banks, which makes her tremble and shake all over, and the whole time the river keeps on rising. The drops of stinking water from the river splash Tacha's wet face, and her two little breasts bounce up and down without stopping, as if suddenly they were beginning to swell, to start now, on the road to ruin.

Webs

Lorne Simon

Survival, when it is strictly only survival, is an ugly thing. Life is something more than just survival. To be alive is to know splendor and beauty. Living is an artform. I am immersed in art. I am forever spinning art from out of my flesh. My purpose in spinning webs is no longer merely to catch flies to eat. There is much more to it now. Indeed, the concern for food becomes incidental to the act of weaving a web. I love the feeling of being lost in abstractions for days at a time, recalculating the design of a work in progress with every shift in the breeze. Marvelous structures are woven and unwoven in my mind as I release filament and descend. Each web is a surprise; I myself never know what shape it will finally acquire. Every moment of creation is also a moment of re-creation, as the slightest changes in meteorology constantly alter and realign variables in physics and geometry. Supports, piers, brackets and braces demand existence in places that I had not imagined would require them.

The weather alters everything.

The finished product, as I have already said is always a surprise. When I complete a web, I stand back into one of its corners and contemplate it, marvelling at the results of a genius that has spontaneously responded to every shift in the elements. I am not boasting. All spiders are possessed when engaged in the act of weaving. We enter a trance and dance with creation. The genius is never ours. We disappear from the world of appetite and enter into pure abstraction. It is never out of egotism that we marvel at our webs. We know that we were only instruments and that the web is a product of something much greater than ourselves.

I never like it when a fly lands on my work too soon after its completion. I need time to concentrate, on the undisturbed web. We believe that in contemplating webs the fullness of appreciation eventually blooms into realizations. Ideally, each web should yield a truth. But life being what it is—so full of chaos and so contrary to design—it is rare that any series of webs will yield their true potential to their creators. More likely than not a fly will crash into the web soon after its completion. How disturbing such moments are! How profoundly disturbing! On the one hand, there is the thrill of catching the next meal and, on the other hand, there is this extreme sense of violation as a part of oneself is rent to threads by the thrashings of a fly.

These moments are disturbing because they overwhelm us with those eternal questions. What is life, if it is not to be in the knowing of wonders? Why, then, does life interrupt itself? Why must the process of knowing be rudely dashed by matters of appetite? Why are not the worlds of appetite and abstraction in harmony? In other words, why does it so rarely happen that a web will remain undisturbed after its completion until it has yielded wisdom to the weaver? Ideally, a fly should land only after that golden moment. This happens by chance every now and again but it is really quite rare. Imagine how wise all arachnids could be!

Perhaps, however, we are not meant to know more than we should. There is a popular horror story told amongst us of a certain spider who once tried a most unusual experiment. He decided to construct three webs in a row. He planned to build the outside ones first and the inside one last. This way he figured the outside webs would shelter the inside one. The webs to the front and the back of the inside web would stop all the flies coming in from both directions. The central web would remain undisturbed and he could contemplate on this web for as long as he pleased. This he did. And when he had completed the project, he set himself on the corner of the inside web and observed. He studied the fascinating weave at his leisure. He sat there for hours and hours and great mysteries were gradually revealed to him. The wonders, however, that the web disclosed eventually trapped him just as surely as webs entangle flies.

He became totally consumed by the outpouring of knowing and he forgot himself. He forgot that he was a spider. He forgot that he had eight legs and a breast full of filament. All the knowing of himself vaporized. Just as he thought he was about to crack the riddle of the universe, a swallow came by and plucked him from his reveries.

I can never forget that story. And sometimes I can't help but think that webs are unnatural. If knowing can only come by fits and starts, then webs are illusions. This artform generates a false sense of completion and harmony. It deceptively suggests to us that it contains the all. In truth, knowing is not so neat and compartmental. Knowing is more like dew. It is everywhere, but it only gathers into little drops that plop off boughs one by one. Yet webs are not altogether deceptive. After all, they elevate the act of survival. Somehow webs prevent life from ever degenerating into ugliness.

EARL YELLOW CALF

JAMES WELCH

Earl Yellow Calf suffered his final stroke in April of the following year. Sylvester had been living in a kitchenette unit in Bismarck and commuting down to the Standing Rock Reservation. The two law students from the University of North Dakota lived in a more modest motel on the western edge of town. He would pick them up every morning at eight and they would drive down the Missouri River through a game preserve, and he always felt the same sense of peace, no matter what the weather. And there were always waterfowl, ducks and geese, sometimes swans and pelicans, cranes and osprey. Deer and antelope watched their car pass with only mild interest. He was always surprised that an area of North Dakota could be so beautiful, so lush and abundant, even in winter. He had driven across the state, east and west, and had thought of it as nothing but wheat fields and prairies. He loved that kind of country and became very attentive in it, as though a discovery would be made over the next hill, down in the next swale or wash. But this country, the slow wide river, the bare trees and brush, the battered reeds and cattails, the bright bunches of willows, held every color, every texture, under the sun or in the snow or rain. Sylvester began to think of the hour-and-a-half drive as his dreaming time. He drove down every morning, and even in the two or three blizzards, as he crept along at thirty, his mind was concentrated on both driving and dreaming, and the things he dreamed were minute and ordinary—times when he was growing up, fishing or shooting baskets, listening to the radiators clank in the old grade school, watching a muskrat preening in the reeds of one of the potholes around Browning. Other times he thought of college in Missoula, the evening walk with the sorority girl, the runs up Mount Sentinel in the fall to get himself in shape for basketball, the smell of pizza in the dorm. He dreamed of Palo Alto and Stanford, the dry hills, the long nights in the law library, the warm early-spring evenings he pedaled home on his bicycle. Even Helena was becoming a dream to him but the dreams did not come as easily. When he dreamed the small bakery that served good bread and soup, he saw faces and he did not want to see faces, so he stopped the dreams and concentrated on the small slick blacktop road or the sudden flight of geese lifting from the wetlands.

In the three months he had been there, he had thrown himself into the case and had gotten a circuit court date for a hearing on the issues, a small triumph in itself. He and the tribal attorney and the two law students spent most of their time researching prior decisions, taking depositions, filing informations, rounding up expert witnesses. Indian irrigators and tribal recreation people were protesting the periodic drawdowns of the immense reservoir, the diversion of water to downstream farmers and ranchers and hydropower concerns. The state maintained that the modification of the prior appropriation law did not apply to this particular case because most of the reservation water was unused. As far as Sylvester could see there were no new wrinkles in either side's arguments; it was simply a matter of convincing the circuit court that the Winters doctrine and later court cases had established that the Indians could protect the amount of water necessary for future as well as current use. But he read all the pertinent water rights cases affecting Indian property. He knew that each case had to be argued on its own particular merits, that it would have to be argued again and again all the way to the Supreme Court if necessary.

At first he didn't know if he wanted to become so deeply involved. It could conceivably take years to settle the case, but the more comfortable he became with the reservation people, the more he got to know the individuals involved, the more he realized he would see it through to wherever it ended—even if it meant giving up his new partnership in Harrington, Lohn and Associates. Lately, it had begun to seem like a small sacrifice.

The telephone call from the priest reached him at the tribal offices in Fort Yates. He and the two student lawyers were eating lunch in the lounge with the recreation specialist. He took the call in the receptionist's area, then called a travel agency in Bismarck.

The next morning he boarded a small commuter plane to Billings, then a Northwest flight to Great Falls. By one o'clock he had rented a car and driven through Great Falls on I-15 on his way to U.S. 89 and Browning. It was April 16th, one day after the tax deadline. His grandfather had died on the 15th. Sylvester smiled as he thought of the irony of the tax deadline and the fact that his grandfather had been an accountant all his working life.

As he approached the Rocky Mountain Front, he noticed that

the country was greening up, even the foothills as they rolled toward the mountains. The fires of last summer had burned through the Scapegoat and Bob Marshall Wilderness Areas but there were no visible scars along the Front. He could barely see the lower slopes of the mountains below the dark clouds. He headed north and west on 89, passing through squall after squall of rain, sleet, and pebbly snow. The area along the Front was the last in Montana to give up winter, forming a natural corridor for weather that began in northern Canada and swept south in massive violent storms. But today the weather consisted of spring squalls, and Sylvester was grateful to be going home in such beauty.

The funeral was in the little Flower Catholic Church in Browning. Although Earl Yellow Calf had not been a church-going man, Mary Bird wanted a church service for him. She had rejected a traditional service because Earl had long ago rejected the traditional way of life. He was a rational man and did not believe in the hocus-pocus, he had once told her.

Sylvester sat in the front row with his grandmother and several of the elders, listening to the organ music, smelling the smoky incense, and staring at the closed casket. Finally, all the shuffling behind him ceased and he glanced back and saw that the church was full. People were standing along the back and side walls. He was both shocked and pleased that his grandfather, his grandparents, had been important in the community they had never left. North Dakota, Bismarck, Standing Rock seemed a long way away, Helena even farther. He had come a long way home to the simplicity and peace of his birthplace.

He wondered if the priest had called his mother in New Mexico. Neither Sylvester nor his grandmother had mentioned her last night, and that seemed to be that. But it was his mother's father lying up there in the casket, and she surely would have come if she had known about it. But there had been no late arrival of a strange woman, a woman who might have looked like Sylvester, a woman who might have touched him like a son. He tried to imagine what she would be doing this spring day in New Mexico, but he couldn't, and he realized that he did not want to see her ever because she might want something from him and he had nothing to give her.

The incense lulled him pleasantly and he thought of Patti Ann Harwood and he realized that in his subconscious he had connected her with the fires of the summer and fall before. Even now he smelled the smoke and saw the orange glow against the night sky. There had been smoke in the air that first morning she came to see him, and all that early fall he smelled it when he stepped from his car in front of her apartment.

He had gotten a letter from her in the middle of February. She thanked him for all he had done for her and her husband. He was now in the Maximum Security Unit, having decided he could live there until his discharge or parole if she would stick by him, be there when he got out. And it wasn't so bad, at least he had peace of mind knowing he would be safe until then. Myrna and Phil were together in Billings at long last, and she, Patti Ann, was plugging away at her job, neither happily or unhappily. She thanked him for their chaste New Year's eve, which meant more to her than he would ever know, and she wished him, belatedly, great success in the new year. She closed with "your loving pal."

The priest gave a short talk, mentioning Carlisle School for Indians, the years put in as tribal treasurer, then as accountant for the BIA, the fact that Earl loved to fish, the many loved ones he left, the respect and esteem of the community toward him. Finally he commended Earl Yellow Calf's soul to heaven and led the throng in a final prayer.

Sylvester sneaked a look at his grandmother. She was smiling.

Hici
Great Aunt Lucy, Oklahoma 1964

Craig C. Womack

"Don't worry, son. Your Aunt Lucille knows what to do when it hurts." I put my arms around his neck, and he lifted me from beneath the covers. I held one hand over my throbbing ear and tensed each time I felt the pulse of pain.

"Sh... Sh...You'll be all right." My Uncle patted my head, and I leaned over and lay against his neck, wiping my tears on his shoulder. "Lucille's already up and sitting in her chair waiting for you. She'll make you better." He patted me on the back again, and, when we got to Aunt Lucy, seated in the kitchen, I unwrapped my arms from around him. She reached out, clutched me, and sat me in the middle of her lap. I turned around to face her while my Uncle left the room.

"Grandson," she said, that's what she called me, and I called them grandma and grandpa. "Listen. I want to tell you the way things are."

I watched her hands, calloused and rough like a man's, always moving while she spoke. She lit the Marlboro and breathed in the smoke, looking past me into the darkness outside the kitchen window. I turned and saw nothing. I bent to the side, turned my face towards her, and she moved close. She breathed deeply, and the red end of the cigarette lit up her face in the dimness. For a moment only, I saw her eyes, brown, nested in furrows, looking straight at me. She exhaled a long stream of smoke into my ear; I felt a hot wave against a bank of pain. Grandma, breathing smoke and stories into me, said, "Mama useta say, *hofónof*, long time ago, that in the beginning it was so foggy you couldn't see nowheres, not even anyone around you."

I felt her legs, so much bigger than mine; her muscles relaxed beneath my fingertips as she began to speak. Grandma pulled me closer, deeper into her lap, until I could feel her breathing in and out, each exhalation in rhythm with her voice. The smoke floated with her words through the kitchen, and a cloud settled around an old tube radio on a high shelf above her head. "Josh, are you listening?" she asked. I stopped tugging on her robe and looked up at her. She continued. "See, a mighty fog had covered us after we'd settled in our new home. You know, we'd just moved there after the earth had opened up and spit us out in the beginning. We'd come a long ways. For a long time we wandered about in darkness. And we all—some way or other out in the dark I s'pose—got lost from one another—couldn't see nothing, and we got real scared. Whenever we heard someone we knew calling, we followed their voice and held fast to that person, so we wouldn't be separated."

I wrapped my arms around her waist until I could feel her flesh beneath the robe. I clasped my hands together behind her back.

"Anyway we stumbled about every which way, forming groups with those we touched. Even the animals were lost, wandering about, making their different cries for help. Bumping and running into each other. Out there in the dark listening to who was in the distance, who was near. The animals had grown so tame—from terror I reckon—that they had no fear of us, and they thronged in with the various bands of people. Many people and animals were wounded and in pain from falling and running into things they couldn't see, and you could hear their voices, full of hurt."

"Did any of the people get bit by the animals?" I asked.

"Quiet, Grandson." She frowned, turning her mouth down and looking straight into my eyes. She pointed out the window. "When the wind swept the fog away, the band of people on the east that first come out of the blackness became the Wind clan. They had no animal near them, but, because they first saw the light, they became the leading clan. So the first animal that the other groups saw, they took the names of whatever birds or animals they found with them when the fog broke. We agreed never to desert our clans. Now, listen to me. The first animal our family spotted was *yaha*, the wolf. We saw him first, so we call him grandfather. When the fog lifted, he was standing in the shadows among the oaks, resting after having loped all frantic-like from the thick haze.

"So it was this here particular wolf who tangled himself in a bramble bush, and his ear was tattered and bleeding. And here we come up the trail, all of us that had joined together in the darkness. When we saw him, trapped in thick vines next to a creek, we helped untangle him. We all held on as gently as we could, one on each leg, one on his back; one held his muzzle shut. The *hilis heyya*, medicine man, spoke words over him, kinda explaining like, so he wouldn't bite or be frightened.

Mama told me, she says 'Lucy,' she always called me Lucy stead of Lucille, says 'Lucy, these are the words we said over wolf':

> on the path he is lying
> stretched out we see him
> he calls out crying
> hurt we see him
> roaming in the darkness we see him
> stretched out we see him
> on the path he is lying

We turned him a-loose, and he stood looking at us before he trotted off into the woods. Remember him always."

I reached up and felt my ear. It still throbbed. "Lean towards me," she said. "One more time and it'll stop hurting." She blew another thin stream of white smoke straight into my ear. I relaxed and turned loose of my grip around her waist, resting my hands in her lap. I watched the dangling gray ashes about to fall from her fingertips.

"Grandmother," I said, "how do you say cigarette?"

"In Creek? *Hici mokkeycka* for cigarette or just *hici* for tobacco."

"Please, one more story. It still hurts."

"This time, Grandson, don't be looking about the kitchen. Put your mind on the story. This one is about your Grandpa when he left Oklahoma for awhile to pick cotton and work in the oil fields in the San Joaquin valley. This happened around Dos Palos, California."

"Where is Dos Palos?"

"It's a flat place with huge fields of alfalfa and cotton, bigger than anything you've ever seen. It's close to a town named Visalia, and a lot of us had to go there and work when our farms went dry. Those of us who hadn't lost them already. Our promised allotments slipped through our fingers when Oklahoma figured out ways to cheat us out of them. So, we made another long trip. Again. We headed west."

"Oh," I said, and listened.

"Anyway, one time the boss-man on one of the ranches your Grandpa worked on—well he had a new Ford coupe—he said to your Grandpa, 'Glen, I want you to clean that car.' So, he did. The work boss had it parked up against an irrigation ditch next to the cotton rows.

"I tell you what," she said. "This ole boy—the boss-man— dipped snuff but he didn't use no can. He spit it right on the floorboard of that new Ford. Like I was saying, he made your Grandpa clean it up."

As she speaks I see Grandpa scrub up the brown stain and wads of shriveled loose-leaf tobacco from the front seat of the car and work like a proud mule that pulls just ahead of the team. The boss-man leans his flesh against the metal of the Ford and guards him. The car is parked up against an irrigation ditch next to the rows of cotton bolls, waving roads of white clouds separated by water. While peering into the window, he opens his mouth and stuffs his cheek full of a large wad, then spits hissing brown streams into the dust at his feet. Meanwhile, Grandpa quietly bends over the floorboard and scrapes, never looking up, dreaming of the dust patch he left that still holds him, its roots burrowing from eastern Oklahoma red clay to San Joaquin valley black silt and surfacing somewhere outside Dos Palos, California, grabbing him by the ankles.

Grandma raised her voice. "Your Grandpa come home and said 'I'm gonna kill that son-of-a-bitch-of-a-boss.' That night he made beans and cornbread for supper and, afterwards, went out back of the tenant house they had for those of us that worked in the fields. It had already gotten dark out. I couldn't see him out there at night, but I could hear the whine of a saw he had brought to California with him, biting into wood. He cut out a beautiful prancing pony from an old piece of plywood and nailed it over the doorway of the shack we useta live in. We still have it. You'll see it from this window when morning comes. We've got it hung on the fence over the garden. In the years that it's been up there, the varnish has dried and cracked, but you can still tell it's a pony."

I looked out the kitchen window and squinted into the darkness, waiting for the first light. I could see Grandpa coming in from his sawing that night, walking in the house, sitting before this woman of shoats and swill and dung and strong hands that had pulled down life from milk-heavy teats. I saw him crawl up onto her lap and clasp stained fingers around her waist while she held onto him in the darkness, lit the Marlboro, and directed wisps of

curling

white

hot

smoke

into his ear. After he straightened his back and pulled himself closer against her, she spoke: "In the beginning we were covered by a mighty fog."

ON OLD 666

CAROL YAZZI-SHAW

It was late at night, and Walter Nez had been driving for hours. The few cars that passed him made him feel glad that he wasn't the only one driving on this narrowback road to Gamerco, New Mexico, out by Gallup. He still had about ninety miles to go, and was very tired. He had gone to Cortez, Colorado, to buy a horse. But when he got there, the only good horses for sale were priced too high. Now he was tired and disappointed.

Walter was in Shiprock, New Mexico, when he stopped at a small cafe for a cup of coffee. After he had two cups, he paid the waitress and started to drive again. Once in awhile he saw lights far away, but he didn't pass any more cars. He reached over to turn on the radio, but there was too much static so he just turned it off.

While Walter was driving he noticed the roadside reflectors. They looked like the shiny lights he saw in his dream the night before. The dream had frightened him. He had always been told that a bad dream meant bad luck, of which he had had enough today. He had dreamt of a car; it was going very fast and he knew that it was out of control as he watched, feeling helpless. In his dream he remembered he was suddenly in the car, and when he tried to step on the brakes, they wouldn't work. He didn't remember the dream very well, but he did remember the young couple—a man and a woman walking by the side of the road. He never saw what that man looked like, but the woman had long black hair that flowed with the breeze and as she looked back at him, she smiled. She was very pale, almost white, and had dark shadows under her vacant eyes and her lips were dark. He yelled out when the car swerved towards the couple as he tried to yank the steering wheel. He was trying to yell when he woke up; he was drenched in sweat and there was a tightness in his chest. He never saw if he hit the couple, but he was terrified and couldn't get the smiling woman off his mind, nor could he get rid of the sad and lonely feeling of remorse inside.

After Walter had driven about twenty miles out of Shiprock, he saw a hitchhiker walking by the road. Walter thought it strange that a person would be hitchhiking on this deserted road and at this time of night. He couldn't remember seeing a broken down car along the road anywhere. When he drove closer, he noticed that the man was wearing his hair in a tsiyeel, a traditional way like many of the young Navajo men today. Walter was tired, and he needed some company so he decided to give the hitchhiker a ride; besides the man was a Navajo like himself. Otherwise, Walter never gave rides to anyone.

Walter stopped several yards in front of the hitchhiker. He looked out the back window, and he could see the man running in the red taillights. He came up to the driver's side of the truck, and Walter rolled down the window.

"Hey man, which way you headed?" the young cowboy asked.

"I'm going to Gamerco. Where are you headed?"

"Oh man, that's great! I'm going to Newcomb," he said.

"Hop in."

The young cowboy threw a bag in the back of the truck. He was young, maybe twenty-three, and was very friendly. When he got in, he reached over to shake Walter's hand.

"*Ya'at'eeh*, Hello," the young man said. "Damn, I didn't think I was going to get a ride."

"How long have you been walking?" Walter asked.

"I was coming from Farmington, and this guy dropped me off a little ways out of Shiprock. He said he lived there somewhere nearby. Then everybody just kept passing me. It sure is hard to get a ride out here."

"Yeah, I'm coming back from Cortez. I went there because a friend of mine said the horses were cheaper out there, but shit, they're more expensive."

"Yeah, I know what you mean. I used to be in the rodeo, and you just can't afford those horses. I used to have a real good horse named Kleedis, but like an asshole I lost it in a bet."

Walter and the hitchhiker had driven several miles when the cowboy took a bottle of Garden Deluxe wine out of his pocket and took a drink.

"Hey, you want a swig? This stuff keeps you awake," he said, laughing.

"No thanks. The doctors told me I'm diabetic so I don't drink anymore. Besides if my wife smells it on my breath, she'll get mad and start throwing things at me," Walter said.

"Shit man, that's a real bummer. I used to have an old lady once—meanest bitch ever bawled for beads," the cowboy said, laughing. "Heard that in a movie once. She was always screwing around so I just left her and her two kids—they weren't mine anyway. Poor kids, she sure was a bitch."

As they drove, they passed a sign that said Sanostee.

"I remember one time when I stopped there," Walter said, pointing at the sign, "these crazy tourists came up to me asking me where the Indians lived so that they could see them do their dances."

"Yeah, so what did you tell them?" the cowboy asked.

"Well, I told them that I was an Indian, and they looked at me real disappointed. So then they asked me, 'What kind of Indian are you?' and I told them that I was a fat brown one," Walter said, looking towards the turnoff as they went by.

The two men laughed.

"Those crazy tourists, man—they'll believe anything you tell them. We used to tell them the Navajo sweat houses were bread ovens like the Pueblos have. We used to tell them that's where we make our fry bread," the cowboy said, laughing.

Before they knew it, they were at Newcomb. Walter pulled off at the trading post and stopped.

"You sure you don't want a snort of this stuff?" the cowboy asked.

"No, but thanks anyway—I have a ways to go yet."

"Well, hey man, thanks!" The cowboy shook Walter's hand and took his bag.

Walter began to drive again. He was close to Sheep Springs and was feeling kinda lonely after dropping off the cowboy, so he began to sing a Nídaa' song, but his heart wasn't in it. He finished the song with an abrupt "Hey'nay yah!" when he saw a Navajo couple walking by the side of the road.

"What the hell are they doing out here?" he said to himself out loud.

The woman was wearing a light sweater and the man a denim jacket. Walter pulled over ahead of them and saw them coming towards the truck. When they came to the door, they just stood there so he opened the door for them

"So where you two headed?" he asked.

But the couple just climbed in and the door slammed shut, so Walter drove off.

When he glanced at them, the woman just sat there with her head down, her long string hair hiding her face. The man was very quiet as he looked out the window.

Walter reached over to turn on the radio, but there was still only static, so he turned it off.

"So where you guys from?" he asked.

They wouldn't answer. Walter was getting nervous. Maybe they're drunk, he thought. Maybe they're fighting. Just my luck. Suddenly the woman began to make whimpering noises. She was hunched over and began to breathe real heavy.

But the woman just kept leaning forward and began to shiver. Walter could feel her trembling next to him. The man just sat there looking out the window.

"Hey man, what's wrong with her? Is she having a baby or something?"

But the man wouldn't move—he just made a moaning sound. The woman was bent over hugging her knees when she began to make a kind of panting sound, and then moaned like she was almost crying.

"What the hell is going on here?" Walter said, when the woman looked up at him and smiled. He let out a gasp in disbelief and shock. Her lips were dark like the shadows under her blank stare and her face was pale. She looked as if she were looking through him as she began to cry. She was the woman from his dream. Walter felt a shudder run through his body and let out a yell as he swerved off the road. All that he saw before he hit his head on the steering wheel was dust everywhere as he tried to slam on the brakes.

When Walter came to, the truck was off in a ditch and the headlights were still on. The passenger door was open, but there was no one around. He had a slight cut on his forehead and was pretty shaken up, but otherwise, he was alright. He got out and spent an hour getting the truck back out of the ditch. He felt very spooked and couldn't stop trembling as he looked around and listened for the strange couple, but there was no one. He felt a weird presence near him, and yet he had never felt so alone, almost like he was in mourning. It was just before dawn when he returned home.

The next day Walter went into work late. He told some people what happened to him that night. There was an old Navajo man standing in the corner listening. Walter had never seen him before. He walked over slowly and said. "You should pick up hitchhikers at night when you're alone."

"I've heard of that couple you're talking about. Other people have seen them. They froze to death by the side of the road a few years ago. They say that no one would pick them up. They keep trying to get a ride, but they never get very far from that place."

A Child's Story

Elizabeth Cook-Lynn

He came slowly, upright and tall in the rich, tooled saddle, smiling just a little in that gentle, knowing way she remembered, careful, graceful, a rhythmic rider, soundless, and inexpressively perfect. He didn't look at her, but she knew that he saw her and was there, in fact, especially because she had come with the child.

She was conscious of the weight of the child as she watched the swinging fringes of his buckskin jacket, back and forth, and she wondered why he was wearing buckskin when it was so oppressively hot. She felt suddenly stifled, like the times she sat in the darkness of Saint Anne's Chapel, felt him close to her, and listened to his soft voice as he sang the white man's religious songs. '

The intransigent heat blurred her vision, and she thought she saw an elk looming beside the mounted figure, yet all she could see of it was the large white eye and then it seemed to fade away.

Her body felt stiff and old.

She watched the motion of the bay horse as it drew nearer. It was a scornful animal, monstrous and solitary, awkward among the other horses, now closed in and stamping, becoming wild in its eyes like a huge bird single-mindedly blinking against the wind. The rider leaned back and then forward with the bay's lunge, and both the man and the horse formed a black, blanketing shadow which she felt upon her. A gust of hot wind, cleanly scented by the buffalo grass of the Dakota prairie ruffled her heavy dark hair, and she thought she heard the words "...whatever is certain..." as if they were carried on the wind.

It seemed to take a long time for the shadow to slowly envelop her. She felt a vague, helpless desire to weep, but she could not. Fascinated, she watched as she let him sweep the child from her arms and begin the ritualistic drama, absorbed in the sound and the motion of it, desolate because she could neither remember nor understand it. She was overcome with a terrible longing for something untraceable from the past, yet he was part of the past. Was her longing for him not over with? Why didn't he leave so that her dignity and calm and serenity could return to her? Her consciousness of the ritual was sharpened by the quick, staccato beat of the bay's hooves upon the hot, hard earth. She tried to utter responses to the ritual, but she could only feel sullen and diffuse and inarticulate as the dust rose around her ankles. Rooted into the wind and the earth, as she supposed she had once been rooted to him, she watched him ride among the other horsemen, who stilled their mounts and gave way for him, their eyes conspiring to see whatever was in the past. And she heard their celebration, "I am the elk." The stamping bay and the tall, male figure held their eyes, and the man held the infant at arm's length, riding around the barren grounds, saying the ageless words which she barely remembered, perhaps never knew.

Inexplicably, idiotically, she felt the unspeakable urge to laugh. For just a moment she was reminded of Father Giesen, that priest at the mission school who always paced between the buildings after the supper hour, reading his breviary in a strident, compelling voice, as though it were not enough to contemplate silently the powers that rested within the words.

But none of the words in either case seemed to make sense. And as she listened, she knew that she could not laugh, as she had not been able to cry.

She felt herself move just a little to the hoofbeats, as if convulsed by the sounds of some far-off drums. She could hear, faintly, the voice of Amos Flying Crow shouting, "*Wacipo...wacipo...!*" and she could almost see him walking around the powwow circle, his arms raised, beckoning the dancers to "come on and dance." And it was then that the memory of them together became intense and the intensity became pain and the pain became anguish. She remembered going slowly around in the dance with him, around the drums and the fires, in time around the drums, together, her heels and his stepping in time, together. She had felt, even then "...whatever is certain...."

The rider kept repeating, "This is my daughter," as he held the infant at arm's length toward the crowd, and the murmurs from the faceless riders affirmed his statement. *Hechetu.*

And then he did the unexpected. He stood up in the heavy stirrups and leaned over as if to help the child reach the ground. The blanket loosened and touched the earth.

No. Wait. She wanted to cry out. But she stood, mute, until she saw the small legs dangling, unable to stand straight, the tiny, moccasined toes involuntarily snubbing back and forth in the dirt. Afraid, her throat hot, she ran forward into the deepened shadow and grasped the child around the belly. She held the infant close and stood motionless, breathless. The face and eyes of the buckskin-clad rider came toward her, and she felt suddenly warm. She caught a sagelike odor from his straight black hair, and she felt helpless for just a moment as the elk-bone ornament tied around his neck swung toward her.

Somehow, with great effort, she stepped back, softly, so that he could not reach her. Her breath came back and her vision was once again momentarily blurred. She could see the dark shape of the man getting darker as his horse stepped sideways, away from her, into the shadow. There was just an instant more when she felt her eyes getting hot and dry, and she felt afraid. But the feeling passed quickly.

Finally, she knew the certainty of "...whatever is certain." The past is always the past as it is always the present.

She heard herself whisper, "Listen! Listen!" into the infant's warm blanket, her ears straining of a stillness she had not known before.

THE BEAR HUNT

LOUIS LITTLECOON OLIVER

A Creek Indian hunter grabbed his bow and arrows and hightailed to bear country, as the season was open to hunt them. A friend in up-state Washington had coached him on how to hunt bears as we don't have them in Oklahoma.

He arrived on the scene of where a giant grizzly had been seen often in a very rugged area. Cautiously he weaved through a thicket where there were signs of fresh bear tracks. He would stop and listen...slithering through tall grass. Once or twice he stopped to let his heart calm down. Suddenly, from behind, a giant black grizzly grabbed him around his chest, a typical bear hug so hard that he could hardly breathe. He had to think quickly as to what to do to try and free himself. Luckily, he had one free hand, so he began to rub the bear's belly. He gradually lowered his rubbing and as he did the monster slackened his hold a bit. He began to fondle his privates which caused the bear to free him and fall backwards flat on his back. The hunter ran as fast as he could until he was nearly fifty yards away. Stopping, he looked to see why the bear didn't chase him. To his surprise he saw it laying flat on its back and motioning him with those giant paws and claws to come back—come back.

Yellow Cat Incident

Louis Littlecoon Oliver

The Okfuske Creek women are a stout lot, the younger generation being tall, lanky and of a complexion without blemish. There were more old maids than usual, but a woman at forty or even at fifty years was considered young. May be that there was a shortage of eligible males that the situation was as it was.

There was a gathering at a house where some kind of activity was going on such as peach peeling or pecan gathering and families came to to help out. At any rate it was a good time for the "old maids" to show-off their physique—their whatever it is that charms a man.

Food had been prepared and it was time to set the table, so to speak. One of the oldest of the maids was known as Hattka, who at this minute was aware of the men folks sitting and watching every move the women made. She decided to make herself more active than the others. She tip-toed, pranced and swayed from kitchen to dining table, putting dishes of things in their proper places. She was putting on a show of grace and beauty to prove to the men that she was without fault. There were two others who were helping with the placing of various dishes and food. While Hattka was in the kitchen, a whole boiled pumpkin had been placed in the center of the table. There was a variety of yellow pumpkin that the Creeks raised and prepared it that way. Hattka came prancing towards the table and saw the yellow pumpkin. She stopped suddenly with raised hands, shouting: "Oh that crazy yellow cat-get off that table! Get off!" She slapped that scalding hot pumpkin and it splattered all over everything on the table.

The men turned their heads and snickered.

Train Time

D'Arcy McNickle

On the depot platform everybody stood waiting, listening. The train had just whistled, somebody said. They stood listening and gazing eastward, where railroad tracks and creek emerged together from a tree-chocked canyon.

Twenty-five boys, five girls, Major Miles—all stood waiting and gazing eastward. Was it true that the train had whistled?

"That was no train!" a boy's voice explained.

"It was a steer bellowing."

"It was the train!"

Girls crowded backward against the station building, heads hanging, tears starting; boys pushed forward to the edge of the platform. An older boy with a voice already turning heavy stepped off the weather-shredded boardwalk and stood wide-legged in the middle of the track. He was the doubter. He had heard no train.

Major Miles boomed. "You! What's your name? Get back

here! Want to get killed! All of you, stand back!"

The Major strode about, soldier-like, and waved commands. He was exasperated. He was tired. A man driving cattle through timber had it easy, he was thinking. An animal trainer has no idea of trouble. Let anyone try corralling twenty-thirty Indian kids dragging them out of hiding places, getting them away from relatives and together in one place, then holding them, without tying them, until train time! Even now at the last moment, when his worries were almost over, they were trying to get themselves killed!

Major Miles was a man of conscience. Whatever he did, he did earnestly. On this hot end-of-summer day he perspired and frowned and wore his soldier bearing. He removed his hat from his wet brow and thoughtfully passed his hand from the hair line backward. Words tumbled about in his mind. Somehow, he realized, he had to vivify the moment. These children were about to go out from the Reservation and get a new start. Life would change. They ought to realize it, somehow—

"Boys—and girls—" there were five girls he remembered. He had got them all lined up against the building, safely away from the edge of the platform. The air was stifling with end-of-summer heat. It was time to say something, never mind the heat. Yes, he would have to make the moment real. He stood soldier-like and thought that.

"Boys and girls—" The train whistled, dully, but unmistakably. Then it repeated more clearly. The rails came to life, something was running through them and making them sing.

Just then the Major's eye fell upon little Eneas and his sure voice faltered. He knew about little Eneas. Most of the boys and girls were mere names; he had seen them around the Agency with their parents or had caught sight of them scurrying behind tepees and teams when he visited their homes. But little Eneas he knew. With him before his eyes, he paused.

He remembered so clearly the winter day, six months ago, when he first saw Eneas. It was the boy's grandfather, Michel Lamartine, he had gone to see. Michel had contracted to cut wood for the Agency but had not started work. The Major had gone to discover why not.

It was the coldest day of the winter, late in February, and the cabin sheltered as it was among the pine and cottonwood of a creek bottom, was shot through by frosty drafts. There was wood all about them. Lamartine was a woodcutter besides, yet there was no wood in the house. The fire in the flat-topped cast-iron stove burned weakly. The reason was apparent. The Major had but to look at the bed where Lamartine lay, twisted and shrunken by rheumatism. Only his black eyes burned with life. He tried to wave a hand as the Major entered.

"You see how I am!" the gesture indicated. Then a nerve-strung voice faltered. "We have it bad here. My old woman, she's not much good."

Clearly she wasn't, not for wood-chopping. She sat close by the fire, trying with a good natured grin to lift her ponderous body from a low seated rocking chair. The Major had to motion her back to her ease. She breathed with asthmatic roar. Wood-chopping was not within her range. With only a squaw's hatchet to work with, she could scarcely have come within striking distance of a stick of wood. Two blows, if she had struck them, might have put a stop to her laboring heart.

"You see how it is," Lamartine's eyes flashed.

The Major saw clearly. Sitting there in the frosty cabin, he pondered their plight and wondered if he could get away without coming down with pneumonia. A stream of wind seemed to be hitting him in the back of the neck. Of course, there was nothing to do. One saw too many such situations. If one undertook to provide sustenance out of one's own pocket there would be no end to the demands. Government salaries were small, resources were limited. He could do no more than shake his head sadly, offer some vague hope, some small sympathy. He would have to get away at once.

Then a hand fumbled at the door; it opened. After a moment's struggle, little Eneas appeared, staggering under a full armload of pine limbs hacked into short lengths. The boy was no taller than an ax handle, his nose was running, and he had a croupy cough. He dropped the wood into the empty box near the old woman's chair, then straightened himself.

A soft chuckling came from the bed. Lamartine was full of pride. "A good boy, that. He keeps the old folks warm."

Something about the boy made the Major forget his determination to depart. Perhaps it was his wordlessness, his uncomplaining wordlessness. Or possibly it was his loyalty to the old people. Something drew his eyes to the boy and set him to thinking. Eneas was handing sticks of wood to the old woman and she was feeding them into the stove. When the fire box was full a good part of the boy's armload was gone. He would have to cut more, and more, to keep the old people warm.

The Major heard himself saying suddenly: "Sonny, show me your woodpile. Let's cut a lot of wood for the old folks."

It happened just like that, inexplicably. He went even farther. Not only did he cut enough wood to last through several days, but when he had finished he put the boy in the Agency car and drove him to town, five miles there and back. Against his own principles, he bought a week's store of groceries, and excused himself by telling the boy, as they drove homeward, "Your grandfather won't be able to get to town for a few days yet. Tell him to come see me when he gets well."

That was the beginning of the Major's interest in Eneas. He

had decided that day that he would help the boy in any way possible, because he was a boy of quality. You would be shirking your duty if you failed to recognize and to help a boy of his sort. The only question was, how to help.

When he saw the boy again, some weeks later, his mind saw the problem clearly. "Eneas," he said, "I'm going to help you. I'll see that the old folks are taken care of, so you won't have to think about them. Maybe the old man won't have rheumatism next year, anyhow. If he does, I'll find a family where he and the old lady can move in and be looked after. Don't worry about them. Just think about yourself and what I'm going to do for you. Eneas, when it comes school time, I'm going to send you away. How do you like that?" The Major smiled at his own happy idea.

There was silence. No shy smiling, no look of gratitude, only silence. Probably he had not understood.

"You understand, Eneas? Your grandparents will be taken care of. You'll go away and learn things. You'll go on a train."

The boy looked here and there and scratched at the ground with his foot. "Why do I have to go away?"

"You don't have to, Eneas. Nobody will make you. I thought you'd like to. I thought—" The Major paused, confused.

"You won't make me go away, will you?" There was fear in the voice, tears threatening.

"Why, no Eneas. If you don't want to go. I thought—"

The Major dropped the subject. He didn't see the boy again through spring and summer, but he thought of him. In fact, he couldn't forget the picture he had of him that first day. He couldn't forget either that he wanted to help him. Whether the boy understood what was good for him or not, he meant to see to it that the right thing was done. And that was why, when he made up a quota of children to be sent to the school in Oregon, the name of Eneas Lamartine was included. The Major did not discuss it with him again but he set the wheels in motion. The boy would go with the others. In time to come, he would understand. Possibly he would be grateful. Thirty children were included in the quota, and of them all Eneas was the only one the Major had actual knowledge of, the only one in whom he was personally interested. With each of them, it was true, he had had difficulties. None had wanted to go. They said they "liked it at home," or they were "afraid" to go away, or they would "get sick" in a strange country; and the parents were no help. They too were frightened and uneasy. It was a tiresome, hard kind of duty, but the Major knew what was required of him and never hesitated. The difference was, that in the cases of all these others, the problem was routine. He met it, and passed over it. But in the case of Eneas, he was bothered. He wanted to make clear what this moment of going away meant. It was a breaking away from fear and doubt and ignorance. Here began the new. Mark it, remember it.

His eyes lingered on Eneas. There he stood, drooping, his nose running as on that first day, his stockings coming down, his jacket in need of buttons. But under that shabbiness, the Major knew, was a real quality. There was a boy who, with the right help, would blossom and grow strong. It was important that he should not go away hurt and resentful.

The Major called back his straying thoughts and cleared his throat. The moment was important.

"Boys and girls—"

The train was pounding near. Already it had emerged from the canyon and momently the headlong flying locomotive loomed blacker and larger. A white plume flew upward—Whoo-oo, whoo-oo.

The Major realized in sudden remorse that he had waited too

long. The vital moment had come, and he had paused, looked for words, and lost it. The roar of rolling steel was upon them. Lifting his voice in desperate haste, his eyes fastened on Eneas, he bellowed: "Boys and girls—be good—"

That was all anyone heard.

THE BLANKET

MARIA CAMPBELL

"I'm glad you believe that, and I hope you will never forget it. Each of us has to find himself in his own way and no one can do it for us. If we try to do more we only take away the very thing that makes us a living soul. The blanket only destroys, it doesn't give warmth. But you will understand that better as you get older."

Cheechum was one hundred and four years old. She was still strong, although her eyesight was failing. She told me that she was getting tired and that she was ready to go at any time. She hoped it wouldn't be too much longer. When we left, she stood outside her little log house and waved—a little lady with long white braids, a bright scarf and long black dress, jewelery on her neck and arms, feet in tiny beaded moccasins.

Daddy came back to Prince Albert with me and made arrangements at the Welfare Department for the children to come to town. Dolores was as tall as I was and looked just like

Mom: she was quiet and gentle. Peggie was barely five feet tall, with red hair and freckles, and a bubbling personality. They were seventeen and fifteen. The little boys had not changed much, only grown a little taller. They cuddled up to me, sang songs, and showed off their magic tricks. They were lonely and wanted so desperately to be loved.

My Cheechum used to tell me that when the government gives you something, they take all that you have in return—your pride, your dignity, all the things that make you a living soul. When they are sure they have everything, they give you a blanket to cover your shame. She said that the churches, with their talk about God, the Devil, heaven and hell, and schools that taught children to be ashamed, were all a part of that government. When I tried to explain to her that our teacher said governments were made by the people, she told me, "It only looks like that from the outside, my girl." She used to say that all our people wore blankets, each in his own way. She said that other people wore them too, not just Halfbreeds and Indians, and as I grew up, I would see them and understand. Someday though, people would throw them away and the whole world would change. I understood about the blanket now—I wore one too. I didn't know when I started to wear it, but it was there and I didn't know how to throw it away. So I understood about those boys' parents—it was easier for them to stay in the car. If they came out from under their blankets, they'd have to face reality, ugly as it was.

The Native movement grew in strength, not just here in Alberta, but across Canada. Community Development, the organization that government had created to keep white radicals busy, suddenly became very threatened. Their objective had been to phase themselves out when Native people no longer needed them. Native people didn't need them anymore and said so. Suddenly their priority became survival. There were thousand-dollar-a-month jobs at stake if these Natives meant business. The Native leaders, whom Community Development had handpicked—and underestimated—would not be dictated to any more. Government, seeing the handwriting on the wall, phased out Community Development and gave us money. Not very much, just enough to divide us again.

The blanket that our leaders almost threw away suddenly started to feel warm again, and they wrapped it tightly around them. Those of us who saw what was happening and spoke out against it were phased out and branded as communists.

One spring day, in May of 1966, I got a phone call from my father. Cheechum had fallen from a runaway horse and buggy and had died almost immediately. He wanted me to come home for the funeral, but I didn't go. All the things that were happening in Alberta were the things she had waited eighty years for, and I knew that she would have wanted me to stay in Alberta and continue working with the movement.

Cheechum lived to be a hundred and four years old, and perhaps it's just as well that she died with a feeling of hope for our people that she didn't share the disillusionment that I felt about the way things turned out. My Cheechum never surrendered at Batoche: she only accepted what she considered a dishonorable truce. She waited all her life for a new generation of people who would make this country a better place to live in.

For these past couple of years, I've stopped being the idealistically shiny-eyed young woman I once was. I realize that an armed revolution of Native people will never come about; even if such a thing were possible what would we achieve? We would only end up oppressing someone else. I believe that one day, very soon people will set aside their differences and come together as one. Maybe not because we love one another, but because we will need each other to survive. Then together we will fight our common enemies. Change will come because this time we won't give up. There's growing evidence of that today. The years of searching, lonelincss and pain are over for me. Cheechum said, "You'll find yourself, and you'll find brothers and sisters." I have brothers and sisters, all over the country. I no longer need my blanket to survive.

HAKSOD

JOHN C. MOHAWK

My car glided silently up the slightly inclined gravel drive, past the great sugar maples that lined the way. He was standing at the edge of his garden, about fifty yards away, leaning against a hoe, facing away from me. Before I was out of the car, he looked my way, his face a smile as I approached.

"Hello," he said, "It's good to see you," his voice flowing with enthusiasm. His name was Harrison Ground, and he had been a chief among the Tonawanda Seneca for some seventy years. He wore a hearing aid, and his body was bent with the weight of more than ninety years. His voice was always soft, and the engaging pools of his grey eyes always seemed somehow placid. He was a pleasant-looking man, slight, given to wearing suspenders, smoking a pipe, and carrying a cane. He was always enthusiastic, always filled with questions about how things were going in the world. One had to remind oneself that seventy years ago this man played professional baseball for a season or two and that as a young man he traveled extensively. Somehow now, it seemed as though he belonged to this place, as though he had never left it, and never would.

We shook hands and stood silently for a moment as we surveyed the garden. It was July, and the rich western New York soil was prolific with plant life. The garden was a marvel for a product of a man and a woman of advanced years. Maybe an acre and a half. There were apple trees to one side, but the main piece was a patchwork of corn and beans and pumpkins, strawberries and beets and radishes. Probably altogether twenty-five or thirty different crops, all in small patches. Corn, potatoes, and beans took up the most room. Harrison and his wife were close to self-sufficient on this small patch, a testimony to the degree of skill and experience they shared.

"Come," he said. "Let's go into the house." We walked around a depression in the soil, some kind of man-made ditch On one side of the ditch I noticed what appeared to be a planting, not in rows, but planted like grain. I stopped next to it.

"Hayug beans," he said. "I still grow some here. Not so many people grow these anymore"' Hayug is a Seneca bean; as far as I know, no one but Seneca grow it. It is used in the summer at the time of the Green Bean Ceremony. A rich and succulent green bean, it always seemed to me a cross between asparagus and a string bean.

My friend and his wife grew most of their food on this small homestead. They had done so most of their lives. They went to the grocery store for sugar and coffee, butter and milk, and the little meat they ate mostly came from the store. But the vegetables and fruits they needed came from their little garden and were stored in the root cellar under their house.

There was usually activity here in the summertime, but never drudgery. They had very little income, yet they typically gave produce away at the end of the summer to people who were hungry. That he and his wife could suffer arthritis and the many infirmities of advanced old age and still raise and preserve so much food on a small piece of land stood as something of a lesson about the advantages of skill over energy and ambition.

Next to the beans was a trellis overgrown with vines. "Those are gourds," he explained. "I make a trellis so the gourds hang free. They grow round that way and are more useful. The gourds aren't eaten. They're prized for the shell which can make dippers or other useful objects, and they're pretty in the garden."

In the house we sat at a table. "I have been thinking about you," and he drew out a pipe from his pocket. "I've been wondering how things are with you."

He had taught me a lot, this old man. He taught me social dance music and ceremonial music. He showed me plants and explained what he knew about the old ways, and he was always helpful, always gentle. I thought I'd come and ask about the old days. "I've been wondering what it was like in the times before, if you knew anybody among our Seneca people who lived before we migrated to this reservation. Did you?" He sat back in his chair a moment, and his eyes seemed to focus on the ceiling above me. After awhile, he put his elbow on the table and rested his chin on his palm.

"When I was a young boy," he began, "I had a friend He was an old man who lived in a cabin in the woods not far from here. Almost every day I went to visit him, and he would invite me inside his little cabin where we would talk On my first visit, when I asked him his name, he said, 'Call me Haksod.' In those times, all the old men wanted to be called 'Haksod.' I had many Haksods when I was a boy.

"Haksod was a very old man. Some people said he was nearly

a hundred years old when I knew him. But wait..." The old man pulled himself up and hurried out of the room, up what I knew to be a staircase. In few moments he was back, carrying a large wooden object.

"You see this?" he asked. He presented an ancient wooden compounder. "Look here," he said. On one side of it were carved two words: Canisteo 1831

Canisteo means Beautiful Corn. It is the name of a Seneca village on the Genesee which was abandoned when people were forced to move westward in the 1830s.

"Our people brought this with them and carved the date on the pounder so we'd remember. This old man, Haksod, was with the people when they moved here."

He stopped for a moment, his voice trailing off. Then, very softly, he started again. "Haksod said that when they were here, in this swamp land, at first it was very dangerous. Everybody had to hide all the time or they might be murdered. Very dangerous. But he said before that, when we lived on the Genesee, it was very pleasant, very nice. He told me once he was born just before the war with Britain.

"He and I were good friends. In those days there was no road to his cabin, just trails in the forest. This was before cars appeared in these parts. Every morning Haksod made mush and tea and cracked corn soup. There were other boys who visited him, too, but I think I visited him the most. He told lots of stories and showed me how to sharpen a knife. I can still remember some of the stories.

"Haksod had friends, old people, when he was young. He could remember talking to people who had been in wars with the French. The Americans. The English. The people he grew up with could remember a long way. Then, one day, it was before noon when I went to his house. It was just a one-room cabin. There were only two windows and a door. I knocked, but no one answered. Finally, I looked through the window, and I could see a figure lying on the cot. So I went in. Haksod lay very quietly. When I touched him, he did not wake. So I ran for help."

Haksod's voice was shaky, even after more than eight decades. "He was the first friend I buried," he said, his voice lowering. "Later, I buried many, but he was the first."

HISTORY

GLORIA BIRD

Dog smell from the blind mutt at his feet envelops him as he shuffles the deck once more. Solitaire and the traps fall one by one as he questions whether a man's destiny is cast before the hand is played out, before the dog will actually die in the house of dust and dim lamps before the man. Or as one day the dog might enter the kitchen pulled by a string of instinct turned dependency to nose the aluminum pie plate set on the floor for him and find it empty. How many hours or days will it take him, the dog, to discover the flimsy shell of the man, his leg stretched out, his foot nosing into the brown gaping mouth of his slipper? Will the dog recognize his master's unmistakable stench of urine and drying feces before howling his hunger others will misconstrue as compassion for the man who fed him but who had often kicked him awake and aside on his way through? The man looks up at nothing, his world a thin caul of yellowing skin filtering the screen of shapes both dark and light

and imperceptible movement. He can smell the distinct sour-
ness of his life, the aching bones of his hands as they lose their
limber and his voice-cracking past. In his thirties a man named
Camille had offered to read him his fortune, swift motions and
expectancy fanned out: great wealth, fame, his name kept within the history books. All lies, of course, but he had believed
them then. All the stories bound up in one flip of a card
Camille had identified as Death, but then he always knew it
would come to this. The great mystery of his life thereafter
hinged upon a name Camille had called him by as he left the
room, had hissed over his shoulder already dismissing him.
Colón. And until this moment the memory of spittle flying
from those curled lips had been long forgotten. He reshuffles
the now softer cards admitting that over the past, say, twenty,
thirty years he has not won one hand. And that lately he
dreams of beautiful, scantily dressed people bearing gifts, but
just as he reaches out to receive them they spill bloodsoaked
into his bed, thud like severed hands. And there are moments
when, like now, he rejects the impossible possibilities. Clearly,
madness and reality, lies and truth are the same thing, the way
his world is now a pantheon of monotonous repetition like
commercials or his frightened prayer mastered through all this
prickling slowed-down time. He is thinking he might believe
again if only he could read if only he could muster the energy it
takes to get up to sluff to the door to retrieve the morning paper
to skim the obituaries for his name to attach to his image this
driving thought of the cumbersome Other which would explain
his disturbed sleep, to put to rest his overwhelming fear, to discover for sure, to have proof and, finally, to know with any certainty at all: were there any survivors?

OH, JUST CALL ME AN INDIAN

DREW HAYDEN TAYLOR

The other day, I, a reasonably well-educated man of the ever-more complex nineties, made a tremendous political and social *faux pas*; I referred to myself and other people of my ethnic background as "Indians."

Oh, the shame of it. You could hear the gasp echo across the room.

It was done, I assure you, with the most innocent intention, but nevertheless, I was soon castigated by both my brethren and, in my humble opinion, the overly politically sensitive members of other cultural groups. And the white people.

Needless to say, in these politically correct times, I was inundated by these same people with criticisms about my use of such an outdated term. "We're/You're no longer called Indians!" I was told over and over again.

Well, I'm evidently severely mistaken in having responded to that term for the past twenty-nine years. No doubt an oversight on my part and that of my entire family and reserve, not to mention the vast majority of the country.

While we were growing up, we were all proud to be "Indians." The word had a certain power to it that set us aside from the white kids. (Or should I say children of occidental descent?)

Somehow the cry of "Proud to be Indigenous Population" just doesn't have the same ring.

Or picture this: You arrive thirsty in some new town, and you ask the first 'skin you see, "Yo, neeches, where's the nearest First Nations Bar?" Sorry—just doesn't work for me.

I guess at twenty-nine I'm out-of-date. Oh, I understand the reasoning behind the hubbub. Columbus, as a member of the European Caucasian nation, thought he found India and so on. That's cool, but there's also another school of thought that says Columbus was so impressed by the generosity and gentle nature of the native population of the Caribbean that he wrote back to Spain saying these people were "of the body of God"—or, in Latin, "*corpus in deo.*" *In deo* equals Indian. A pretty thin link, but who knows? I know some Indians with God-given bodies.

But a person in my position doesn't have time to defend himself with theoretical history. Since my *faux pas*, I've been too busy handling the deluge of politically correct terms I am permitted and urged to use.

It must be obvious to most people that in the past few years, native people in Canada have gone through an enormous political metamorphosis, similar to that of people of African descent. Years ago they used to be called niggers, then Negro, then colored, then black and finally, today, I believe the correct term is African-American or African-Canadian.

That's nothing to the selection of names and categories available to the original inhabitants of this country. And these names or classifications have nothing to do with any tribal affiliations—they're just generic terms used to describe us "Indians."

Grab some aspirin and let me give you some examples. We'll start with the basics: status, nonstatus, Metis. So far, painless. I guess next would come the already mentioned Indian, fallowed by native, aboriginal, indigenous and First Nations. Pay attention, there's going to be a test afterward. From there we can go to "on-reserve," "off-reserve," urban, treaty.

Got a headache yet? How about the enfranchised Indians, the Bill C-31 or reinstated people, the traditional Indians, the assimilated Indian? I'm not finished yet.

There are the wannabes (the white variety), the apples (the red variety), the half-breeds, mixed bloods and, of course, the ever-popular full bloods.

My personal favorites are what I call the Descartes Indians: "I think Indian, therefore I am Indian."

Get the picture? Right—there are a couple of dozen separate names for our people. Where does it all stop? I want to know just who keeps changing all the rules.

Even I get confused sometimes. That's why I usually use the term "Indian." I'm just too busy or too lazy to find out which way the political wind is blowing, or to delve deeply into the cultural and government background of whomever I'm talking or writing about. By the time I go through all the categories, I've missed my deadline. Then I become an unemployed Indian.

But I know what you're thinking. Why should I listen to the guy? What the hell does he know? He's probably just some status, off-reserve, urban, native, aboriginal, treaty, half-breed Indian. Well, this week, anyway.

Tahotahontanekentseratkerontakwenhakie

Sally Benedict

Deep in the woods, there lived a man and his wife, and their newborn baby boy. The baby was so young that his parents had not yet given him a name. Hunting was very bad that winter and they had very little to eat. They were very poor.

One day around suppertime, a little old man came to their door. He was selling rabbits.

"Do you wish to buy a rabbit for your supper?" he asked.

The woman who met him at the door replied that they were very poor and had no money to buy anything.

It was growing dark and the man looked very tired. The woman knew that he had traveled very far just to see if they would buy a rabbit from him. She invited him to stay for supper and share what little they had to eat.

"What is your name?" the husband asked as he got up to meet the old man.

"I have no name," the little man replied. "My parents were

146

lost before they could name me. People just call me Tahotahontanekentseratkerontakwenhakie which means, 'He came and sold rabbits.' "

The husband laughed. "My son has not been named yet either. We just call him The Baby."

The old man said, "You should name him so that he will know who he is. There is great importance in a name." The old man continued, "I will give you this last rabbit of mine for a good supper, so that we may feast in honor of the birth of your new son."

In the morning, the old man left. The parents of the baby still pondered over a name for the baby.

"We shall name the baby after the generous old man who gave him a feast in honor of his birth."

"But he has no name," the mother said.

"Still, we must honor his gift to our son," the husband replied. "We will name our son after what people call the old man, Tahotahontanekentseratkerontakwenhakie which means, 'He came and sold rabbits.' "

"What a long name that is," the mother said. "Still, we must honor the old man's wish for a name for our son and his feast for our son."

So the baby's name became Tahotahontanekentserat-kerontakwenhakie which means, "He came and sold rabbits," in honor of the old man.

The baby boy grew older and became very smart. He had to be, to be able to remember his own name. Like all other children he was always trying to avoid work. He discovered that by the time his mother had finished calling his name for chores, he could be far, far away.

Sometimes his mother would begin telling him something to do, Tahotahontanekentseratkerontakwenhakie...hmnnm... She would forget what she wanted to have him do, so she would smile and tell him to go and play.

Having such a long important name had its disadvantages too. When his family traveled to other settlements to visit friends and other children, the other children would leave him out of games. They would not call him to play or catch ball. They said that it took more energy to say his name than it did to play the games.

News of this long, strange name traveled to the ears of the old man, Tahotahontanekentseratkerontakwenhakie.

"What a burden this name must be for a child," the old man thought. "This name came in gratitude for my feast for the birth of the boy. I must return to visit them."

The old man traveled far to the family of his namesake, Tahotahontanekentseratkerontakwenhakie. The parents met the old man at the door and invited him in. He brought with him food for another fine meal.

"You are very gracious to honor me with this namesake," he said. "But we should not have two people wandering this world, at the same time, with the same name. People will get us confused, and it may spoil my business. Let us call your son Oiasosonaion which means, 'He has another name.' If people wish to know his other name, then he can tell them."

Oiasosonaion smiled and said, "I will now have to call you Tahotahontanekentseratkerontakwenhakie tenon Oiasahosonnon which means, 'He came and sold rabbits and gave the boy another name.'"

Everyone laughed.

CHE

ANNA LEE WALTERS

A stretch of high empty plains rolled up to touch the sky in Canada somewhere, a few miles north. The late summer sky was a pale afternoon blue. Tall yellow grass made scratching sounds as it was pushed underfoot. Stella wore cowboy boots; they followed Jim's steps.

"See anything yet?" she asked him in a soft southern drawl. He shook his head no and raised the cowboy hat on his head back an inch or two while he chewed on a long stem of grass. They continued to walk northward in a heavy silence. Their pickup truck, parked behind them, grew smaller and smaller. They walked further into the high grass, their legs sinking into it, into the silence that was magnified out there. The wind occasionally beat the grass and it rippled, sending wave after wave to Canada.

The landscape looked flat to the two people, but actually they were climbing a slope. They were in no hurry and took their time. When the wind pushed on their backs, moving gently north, they didn't resist. They were guided by it.

Jim turned to Stella and said skeptically, "The old people always say, *This place was black with buffalo once*. I, myself, often wondered."

Stella stopped where she stood and looked arund. "Yu mean right here, Jim?" she asked.

"Yeah," he said, still chewing the long stem. "Our people tell about it all the time. It's an obsession with them I think—the buffalo."

"My people's the same way, Jim. They were like that too. You know, up until two generations ago, they still chased buffalo all through Nebraska. Couldn't seem to forget *che* afterward. I'm not sure they have yet, even with new generations since," she said.

Jim nodded, took Stella's hand. "Hon,," he said, "I'll tell you something, a secret I've never told anyone. There have been times when I've doubted that the buffalo and the buffalo people ever existed. I think it was a figment of someone's imagination."

Stella laughed and asked, "Well, are you saying that the 'coming of the whiteman' was part of that imagination? I mean, after all, he's here."

Their steps carried them furthr up the slope, following the flow of windy waves that rippled grass northward. Jim spit and said, "Your knkow what I mean. I don't think it's true. I've seen nothing of those times, but ehe people persistently claim it was so. They tell stories of shaggy, wonderful beasts and tireless peopl.e who chsed them. Our people sound so childish with those tales. No one takes them seriously anymore. You know, the few buffalo I've seen are pitiful creatures over on the protected range. hard to believe that they're the same ones, the sacred animals the people talk about."

Jim turned toward their vehicle. It was a sliver of metal that gave off such a blinding reflection in the sun that Jim winced.

"Over here somewhere there should be rocks, a line of rocks, if what they say is true. And there should be another on the west rim over there," he pointed. Stella raised her hand to shade her eyes and looked west, just below the sun.

The top of the ridge was still a good distance away. Jim slowed his pace. His eyes scoured the high grass for a hidden line of rocks, but none were visible. He strode in circles for a while, moving the shrubbery and undergrowth with his boots, but his search went unrewarded.

"You think everything's gone by now?" Stella asked. The grass danc ed around her knees under a low, moaning wind. "I mean, you've said before that the last time this particular jump was used was nearly two hundred years ago, didn't you? Is that true?"

"I don't know, except that it was in use for a good five hundred years at least. There should be *something* here." He was almost angry as he said the words. "Damn! I didn't believe it anyway."

The grass undulated southward and then north as he spoke. The wind flapped Stella's long hair over her shoulders, and Jim's shirt collar blew up and tuched his ears.

He walked away frm Stella and began to stomp the grass down arund the thick undergrowth near him. Againhe found nothing. Stella stood where she was, trying to imagine the empty plain covered with illusive buffalo.

"There's nothing here," Jim conceded. He *was* angry, she could tell. "Let's head on back," he continued. "It was a figment of someone's imagination. No buffalo, no buffalo people. There's just now. We've never been anything but what we are now."

Jim's anger confused Stella. "Why are you mad, Jim?" she asked with a slight frown.

He ansered, "I'm not mad, just disappointed, I guess." He yanked his cowboy hat off his head and slapped it against his leg.

His shoulder-length hairswirled around his head.

"Do you want to find it, Jim, or are yu afraid to find it?" Stella saked in a low, barely audible voice.

Jim glared at her. "I'm here, aren't I?" he said. "Chasing buffalo that's long gone or never existed!"

Stella wasn't through talking though. "Maybe we'd rather not know for ourselves if there's anything to all these stories. If we find it, it means the old people know what they've been talking about. It means that life wasn't always what it is now. If we don't find it and this is where it's supposed to be, then the old people are fools perpetuating an older lie that someone started a really long time ago. Either way, it means facing something square in the face."

Jim's expression softened. Looking around him, he answered, "Well, one thing's certain. The earth is as they said—it's beautiful out here. Nothing to stand between you and the Maker. It almost makes me believe there is a Maker somewhere...but I doubt it." The wind tousled his black hair again. He combed it down with his free hand and smashed the hat back on his head.

"Come on," Stella said, "we got time. Let's look around." She held out her hand, and Jim walked to her and put his hand around hers. The two people were simply specks on the land from the distance of their truck.

"You know," she said to Jim after they had walked for some time, "being out here brings back some things I had forgotten since I was a child."

"What's that?" he asked.

"Well, one of my grandmother's names had to do with buffalo. She was a little girl and you know how children are, playing all the time and getting dirty and dusty as quick as they can. My grandmother was like that, I guess. Her girlhood name was Covered With Buffalo Dust. Can you imagine a name like that?

Later she took a regular name." Stella frowned as she added, "She's dead now, Jim."

The wind's sound grew, and Jim threw an arm over Stella's shoulders. "There's something else too," the woman told him. "I remember a song about buffalo. It called the buffalo by name. Know what it was?"

Jim shook his head no.

"The song said the buffalo's name was Grandfather. I never understood it," Stella confessed.

Jim didn't answer. He was absorbed in his thoughts. The two moved as one across the earth in solitude. Only the moaning wind spoke.

Unexpectedly Jim found himself studying a broken line of boulders, running south to north, covered with patches of black and orange lichen. He stopped. Stella lifted her boot and rested it on the largest spongy boulder. "You think this is it, Jim?" she asked. Her eyes were strangely lit in excitement.

He didn't answer but followed the line northward. Other boulders lay scattered on both sides of it.

"How does the story go again, Jim?" Stella asked.

"Well, supposedly these walls were to keep the buffalo running in the direction the people wanted them to go. Men were stationed behind them or along them. They say these walls were built up pretty high so the buffalo wouldn't go over them, but had to turn...that way." He pointed to the ridge.

Jim and Stella stood there momentarily looking toward the jump. Then she yelled, "I'll race you to it!"

They began to run toward the jump, panting softly, sounding like the wind themselves. In a few minutes they were at the site. Breathlessly she threw herself down on the ground and gasped for air. The land under them dropped abruptly in a deadly fall of several feet. Below that, the earth smoothly folded into a steep ravine.

"Canada begins right there," Jim told her, "where the land meets the sky." He took off his hat again, shook his head, and squashed the hat down on his head once more. The wind grew around them, rustling the tall grass and the clothing they wore. Jim climbed down the drop and began to scout around.

"What are you looking for?" Stella called to him over the wind.

"The place where the holy person stood," he yelled back at her. "He waited below the ridge and it was he who called the buffalo here." His words were tossed in the wind.

Stella pulled herself up and followed. They wandered around until Jim discovered a hollowed out space in the ground, just under the drop. There was a wall of rocks around the indentation. "Here it is," Jim said. He stepped into a space just wide enough for a man to sit or stand.

"What did he do here?" Stella asked.

"I don't really know. Prayed, sang. But he waited here, calling the buffalo over the ridge in some mysterious way. The other people, the hunters, were on top, back there," he pointed up to the ridge. "They got the buffalo to run, to charge as fast as they could, between the line of rocks and men up there. By the time the herd reached the ridge, there was a cloud of dust, and the buffalo fell down here." He pointed again, to the ravine. The wind moaned loudly.

Stella's eyes followed his hand to the spot below them. She was strangely quiet, and so was he after he described the killing. He sat down in the narrow space of the ancient shelter. When she saw that he wasn't going to budge for a while, she walked toward the ravine.

The wind calmed in the jagged ravine, a dramatic contrast to the moaning on the hill. Stella made her way through the abundant brush and found herself in a small clearing. Bright-colored pebbles were generously scattered over the earth. She looked up to Jim, still holding the same position. His eyes narrowed and focused toward Canada.

Stella took off the cowboy shirt she wore over her T-shirt. She threw it down on the ground and sat on it. Then she pulled off one boot at a time. She lay down on one arm and looked back up toward Jim, wondering what he was thinking. He had not moved. The sun was poised on the hill southwest of Jim, while puffs of clouds sailed over the ridge to Canada.

She lay in a fold of the earth. The brush encircling the clearing made noises as birds dove into it. Peace and quiet reigned where hundreds of buffalo once fell. That thought stayed with her. She wanted to close her eyes.

Several minutes elapsed with Jim still lost in his own reverie. He paid no attention to Stella.

She dreamed of thunder rolling over her. Of dark clouds blown from the earth up to the sky. Of choking, blinding dust, and a hot, charging wind. A rumbling on the ridge above Jim. He'd called them with a name. The cloud on the ridge emitted a thundering sound and the earth trembled. She felt it beneath her bones.

Jim shook her. He said, "Let's go back. There's nothing here." Startled, she sat up and looked around. The jump was quiet, the earth so still.

"Jim," she said, "I had a strange little sleep. I dreamed of something coming, no running, to the edge of the jump up there. Buffalo, I think. *Che.* I never saw them, but they were so close that I heard them and felt them. I think I even smelled them."

She began to pull her boots on while Jim said, "It's your imagination. This place got to you, that's all."

She shook her shirt and put it back on. "Jim," she insisted, "I could swear there were buffalo here!"

Jim spread his arms to indicate the space around him, "Do you see anything?"

Stella shook her head and said, "No, but that doesn't mean much. I was going to look around before I went to sleep. I'm not ready to go yet." She hurried away from Jim and disappeared into the brush.

Jim decided to humor her and waited patiently, sitting in the dirt and tossing pebbles at the birds diving into the brush. She returned in a few minutes. Jim asked her, "Find anything?"
Her answer was no. They began to climb back up toward the jump. They took a different route than the one they had followed down. Stella's eyes stayed on the ground, seeking a fragment of time, of something old and hidden that only they could spot.

"Look, I didn't know you were going to be fanatic about this," Jim laughed.

Stella replied, "I guess I might be silly at that. It's just that they were so close, I could feel their breath. It felt like the wind."

The heel of her boot caught itself in the cracked ground. She lifted her leg, and the heel imprint was stamped in the sandy wash. Then it sifted slowly into the earth. She knelt down to scratch the dirt with her fingernails. Jim watched her, entranced by her new behavior.

"It's here!" she told him excitedly.

"What?" he asked calmly.

"Bones," she said, "they're underneath."

Jim wore an amused expression. "You're kidding!" he said. "No," she answered, her fingers digging rapidly, throwing dust. She dug for several minutes until her hands were bruised and scratched, and dusty to the wrists. She brushed dirt from a smooth white porous surface that appeared.

"There!" she said. She stopped digging and looked up at Jim. His expression was hard to read. "See Jim, there's buffalo here!" She twisted her hair back when it began to fly around her face and left a streak of dirt on her forehead and chin.

Jim laughed at her, and himself, chasing buffalo this way. Stella understood and laughed too. She added, "Buffalo people, too!"

Jim pulled her up, threw an arm over her shoulder, and guided her toward the rim of the jump. At the top they surveyed the ravine again. Stella turned to Jim. Before she could speak, Jim said to her, "You're all dusty."

She answered, "It's buffalo dust, Jim. We're all buffalo dust. I finally understand."

Jim asked, "Understand what?"

"The song," she said. The wind moaned everywhere. "The buffalo people live on, Jim. The buffalo may be gone or may be penned up on some protected range. But their bones and ours are the same. That's why the people keep the buffalo alive. Feed the stories of che to us."

"When I was sitting down on the ledge where the holy person sat," Jim responded. "I had a strange feeling that if I called the buffalo here, they would come. I had a silly urge to try. But then I didn't know what to say and the feeling went away. I guess it's the buffalo man in me. I didn't know it was there." He laughed.

The two people turned and began their trek to the pick-up truck. It was a long way. The sun was setting on them and the buffalo jump.

Stella turned to Jim. The plain was still, without a ripple of wind then. "It's beautiful here," she said, "but you know what's best of all about this?" Jim gave a parting look at the jump and did not answer.

Stella answered her own question. "That it exists. Amid the skyscrapers, space shuttles, the computers. This place exists untouched and will, as long as we hide it and remember that it's here."

Jim was absorbed in his own thoughts. He turned to Stella and said, "This place was black with buffalo once." He waved his hand over the plain. As they walked to the truck, she answered, "*Che*." It echoed in the silence there.

Che is Otoe for buffalo.

HIS WIFE HAD CAUGHT THEM BEFORE

LESLIE MARMON SILKO

His wife had caught them together before
and probably she had been hearing rumors again
the way people talk.

It was early August
after the corn was tall
and it was so hot in the afternoon
everyone just rested after lunch
or took naps
waiting for evening when it cools off
and you can go back to weeding
and working in the fields again.

That's what they were counting on—
this man and that woman—
they were going to wait
until everybody else went
back up to the village for lunch
then they were going to get together
down there in the corn fields.
That other woman was married too
but her husband was working in California.
This man's wife was always
watching him real close at night
so afternoon was
the only chance they had.

So anyway
they got together there
on the sandy ground between the rows of corn
where it's shady and cool
and the wind rattles the big corn stalks.

They were deep into those places where people go
when this man's wife showed up.
She suspected she would find them together
so she brought her two sisters along.
The two of them jumped up
and started putting their clothes back on
while his wife and his sisters-in-law
were standing there saying all kinds of things
the way they do
how everyone in the village knows
and that's the worst thing.

So that other woman left
and it was just this poor man alone
with his wife and his sisters-in-law
and his wife would cry a little
and her sisters would say
                    "Don't cry, sister, don't cry,"
And then they would start talking again
about how good their family had treated him
and how lucky he was.

He couldn't look at them
so he looked at the sky
and then over at the hills behind the village.
They were talking now

what a fool he was
because that woman had a younger boyfriend
and it was only afternoons that she had any use
for an old man.

So pretty soon he started hoeing weeds again
because they were ignoring him
like he didn't matter anyway
now that
that woman was gone.

Then there was the night
old man George was going
down the hill to the toilet
and he heard strange sounds
coming from one of the old barns
below.
So he thought he better
check on things
just in case some poor animal
was trapped inside—
maybe somebody's cat.
So he shined his flashlight inside
and there was Frank—
so respectable and hard-working
and hardly ever drunk—
well there he was
naked with that Garcia girl—

you know,
the big fat one.
And here it was

the middle of winter
without their clothes on!

Poor old man George
he didn't know what to say
so he just closed the door again
and walked back home—
he even forgot where he was going
in the first place.

SHE SITS ON THE BRIDGE

LUCI TAPAHONSO

When Nelson was still running around and drinking years
ago, he was coming home from Gallup
hitch-hiking late at night
and right by Sheepsprings Trading Post—
you know where the turn to Crystal is?
Well, he was walking near there
when he heard a woman laughing somewhere nearby

It was dark there
(there were no lights at the trading post then)
he couldn't see anyone but he stopped and yelled out
        Where are you? What happened to you?
but she kept laughing louder and louder
and then she started to cry in a kind of scream.

Well, Nelson got scared and started running
then right behind him—he could hear her running too.
Sbe was still crying and then he stopped   she stopped also.

She kept crying and laughing really loud
coming behind him and she caught up with him.
He knew even if he couldn't see her.
She was gasping and crying
right close to him—trying to catch her breath.

He started running again faster and off to the side
he saw some lights in the houses against the hill
and he ran off the road towards them then
then she stopped and stayed on the highway
still laughing and crying very loudly.

When Nelson got to the houses
he heard people laughing and talking
they were playing winter shoe games inside there.
But a little ways away was a hogan with a light inside
he went there and knocked
Come in   a voice said
An old man (somebody's grandpa) was there alone
and upon seeing him said
      Come in!   What happened to you?
and started to heat up some coffee.
Nelson told the old grandpa about
the woman crying on the road.

     You don't know about her? he asked.
     She sits on the bridge sometimes late at night.
     The wind blows through her long hair.
     We see her sitting in the moonlight or
     walking real slow pretending to be going to Shiprock.
     We people who live here know her and
     she doesn't bother us.
     Sometimes young men driving by pick her up—
     thinking she wants a ride and after riding a ways
     with them—she disappears right in front of them.
     She can't go too far away, I guess.

That's what he told Nelson
stirring his coffee.
Nelson stayed there in the hogan that night and the old
grandpa kept the fire going until morning.

THE PANTHER WAITS

SIMON J. ORTIZ

"That people will continue longest in the enjoyment of peace who timely prepare to vindicate themselves and manifest a determination to protect themselves whenever they are wronged."
—Tecumseh, 1811

Tahlequah is cold in November, and Sam, Billy, and Jay sat underneath a lusterless sun. They had been drinking all afternoon. Beer. Wine. They were talking, trying not to feel the cold.

Maybe we need another vision, Billy.

Ah shoot, vision. I had one last night and it was pretty awful—got run over by a train and somebody stole my wife.

He he he. Have another beer, Billy.

Maybe, though, you know. It might work.

Forget it, huh. Cold beer vision, that's what I like.

No, Sam, I mean I've been thinking about that old man

166

that used to be drunk all the time.

Your old man, he he he, he was drunk all the time.

Yeah, but not him. He was just a plain old drunk. I mean Harry Brown, that guy that sat out by the courthouse a lot. He used to have this paper with him.

Harry J. Brown, you mean? He was a kook, a real kookie kook, that one?

Yeah. Well, one time me and my brother, Taft, before he died in that car wreck down by Sulphur, well, me and him we asked Harry to buy us some beer at Sophie's Grill, you know, and he did. And then he wanted a can and sure, we said, but we had to go down by the bridge before we would give him one. We did and sat down by the bushes there and gave him a beer.

Yeah, we used to, too. He'd do anything for a beer, old Harry J. Brown. And your brother, he was a hell of a drinker, too, he he he.

We sat and drank beer for a while, just sitting, talking a bit about fishing or something, getting up once in a while to pee, and just bullshitting around. And then we finished all the beer and was wishing we had more, but we had no money, and we said to Harry, Harry, we gotta go now.

He was kind of fallen asleep, you know, just laid his head on his shoulder like he did sometimes on the cement courthouse steps. We shook his shoulder.

Uh, uh yeah, he said. And then he sort of shook his head and sort of like cleared his eyes with his hand, you know, like he was seeing kind of far and almost like we were strangers to him, like he didn't know us, although we'd been together all afternoon.

We said we was leaving, and he looked straight up into Taft's eyes and then over to me and then back to Taft. And then he rubbed his old brown hand over his eyes again and said, Get this. He said, Yes, kinda slow in his voice and careful, Yes, it's true, and it will come true.

I just realized, Harry Brown said slowly but clearly then, not like later on when you'd hardly understand what he was saying at the courthouse.

Realized, he repeated, you're the two. Looking straight into Taft's and my eyes. And then he kind of smiled and made a small laugh and then he shook and started to cry.

Harry, Taft said, you old fool, what the hell you talking about. C'mon, get a hold of yourself, shape up, old buddy. Taft always liked to talk to old guys. Sometimes nobody else would talk to them or make fun of them, remember? But Taft was always buddies with them.

Yeah, they gave him wine, that wino, Sam giggled. He knew how to hit them up.

Anyway, Harry sat up then and didn't look at us no more, but he said, Sit down, I want to show you something. And then he pulled out this paper.

It was just a old piece of paper, sort of browned and folded, soft-looking, like he'd carried it a long time. Listen, he said, and then he didn't say anything. And we said again, We gotta go soon, Harry.

Wait. Wait, he said, you just wait. It's time to wait. And so we kept sitting there, wondering what in the world he was up to. The way Harry Brown was, his eyes sort of closed and thinking, made us interested.

Finally, he cleared his throat and spit some beer foam out and then he said, I just remembered something I thought I forgot. It's not from a long time ago, I don't think but longer than a man's age, anyway. I'm maybe seventy years along and that's not too long and what I remembered is longer than that. I carry this with me all the time. Once I thought I lost it, but then it had got thrown in the washing machine by Amy, my daughter, and she pulled it out of my pants, and you can't tell what it says clearly, but it's there, and it will always be there. I can still see it.

And then Harry opened up the paper. There was nothing on it, just a brown piece of wrinkled paper. There's nothing there, Harry, I said, nothing but a piece of paper.

There's something there, he said, serious and solemn. There's something there. It's clear in my mind.

I looked over at Taft, who was on his knees staring at the paper and he caught my eye. I kind of shrugged, but Taft didn't say anything. I knew old Harry Brown's mind probably wasn't all that clear anymore with his old age and all the wine he drank all the time. But you know, he spoke clearly, and the way he was talking was serious and sure.

He said, They traveled all over. They went south, west, north, east, all those states now that you learn about in books. Even Florida, even Mississippi, even Missouri, all over they did.

Who did? Taft asked. I was wondering myself.

The two brothers. Look, you can see their marks and their roads. He was pointing with his shaky old scarred finger. That old man had thick fingers. I've seen him lift a beer cap off the old kind of beer bottle with his thumb. The scar was from when the state police slammed his hand some years ago.

Taft was looking at the paper with a curious look on his face. I mean curious and serious, too. I still couldn't see anything. Nothing. I thought maybe there was a faint picture of something, but there didn't seem to be anything—just paper.

Taft looked over at me then and made a motion with his chin, and I looked at the paper again and listened.

They tried to tell all the people. They said, You Indians—they meant all the Indians wherever they went and even us now I'm sure—you Indians must be together and be one people. You are all together on this land. This land is your home and you must see yourself as all together. You people, you gotta understand this. There is no other way we're gonna be able to save our land and our people unless we decide to be all together.

The brothers traveled all over. Alabama, Canada, Kentucky, Georgia, all those states now on the map. Some places people said to them, We don't want to be together. We're always fighting with those other people. They don't like us and we don't like them. They steal and they're not trustworthy.

But the brothers insisted, We are all different people, that's for sure, but we are all human people, all humankind, all sisters and brothers, and this is all our land. We have to settle with each other No more fighting, no more arguing, because it is the land and our home we have to fight for. That is what we have come to convince you about.

The brothers said, We will all have to fight before it's too late. They are coming. They keep coming and they want to take our land and our people. We have told them, No, we cannot sell our mother earth, we cannot sell the ocean, we cannot sell the air, we cannot give our lives away. We will have to defend them, and we must do it all together. We must do it, the brothers said. Listen.

Taft just kept looking at the paper and the brown finger of Harry Brown moving over the paper, and I kept looking, too. I still didn't see anything except the wrinkles and folds of the paper, but what Harry was saying with his serious-story voice put something there I think, and I looked over at Taft again. He was nodding his head like he understood perfectly what the old man was saying.

They were talking about the Americans coming and they wanted the Indians to be all together so they could help each other fight them off. So they could save their land and their families. That's what I remembered just awhile ago. I thought

I'd forgotten, but I don't think I'll ever forget. It's as close to me as you two are.

Harry paused and then he went on. They were two brothers like you are. One of them, the older, was called Tecumtha. I've heard it means *the panther in waiting*. And the other was one who had old drunk problems like me, but he saved himself and helped his people. Maybe the vision they said he had came from his sickness of drinking, but it happened and they tried to do something about it. That's what is on here, look.

And Taft and I looked again, but I still couldn't see anything. But I didn't say so, and Taft said, Yeah, Harry, I see.

And then we had to go. We was supposed to pick up some bailing wire from Stokes' Store and take it back to our old man. Before we left, Harry looked up at us again, straight into our faces. His eyes had cleared, you know, and he said, They were two brothers.

Taft and I talked some about it and then later on somebody—you know Ron and Jimmy, the two brothers from up by Pryor.

Yeah, Jimmy the all-state fullback, Boy, was he something. Yeah, I know them.

Yeah. Well, Ron told me old Harry Brown told them that same story, too. but they couldn't see nothing on the paper, either. They said it was kind of blue not brownish like I'd seen. I told Taft and he said, Well those two guys are too dumb and ignorant to see anything if it was right in front of their nose.

Jimmy got a scholarship to college and works for an oil company down in Houston, and Ron, I think, he's at the tribal office, desk job and all that, doing pretty good. I said to Taft, You didn't see anything, either. And he looked at me kind of pissed and said, Maybe not, but I know what Harry meant.

Geesus, that Taft could drink. He coulda been something, too, but he sure could drink like a hurricane, he he he. Tell us again what happened, Jay.

No, Sam, it was just a car wreck.

Maybe we need another vision, Billy said.

PIEGAN STILL LIFE

STEPHEN GRAHAM JONES

The 30.06 was a loaner that got out of hand, was supposed to have been driven down to Great Falls by the end of November, no later. But then the real cold didn't come, so the elk had no real reason to come down from Glacier, and the one time they tried Jayare chased them back over with what sounded like a bazooka then returned to his desk and signed out permits with a smile pulled across one side of his face, reaching for an ear gone deaf by the chase. The 30.06 was supposed to have been a week-end deal, but then the week-end lasted a month. And no elk. One cow moose—or, moose cow, as Aiche (not his real name) called them, lowing like beef—but then Nat thought that maybe he might possibly have seen the glint of a bumper or windshield on their backroad, meaning the moose by that point in the conversation was half-quartered, steaming, abandoned. When Aiche returned that night minus headlights and plus beer, there was nothing, drag marks and twin tire tracks,

173

and he toasted whoever the glint had been.

The 30.06 as Aiche passes the Great Falls city limit sign is nosed behind the accelerator. Behind the seat would be better since there's paraphernalia but the seat doesn't lean up anymore, due to the chainsaw Nat the genius wedged back there, the pullcord down by the lap belt, a joke in the making: Nat running off into Starr School, Aiche diving from the truck, the chain sparking on the gas tank, the truck coughing itself empty fifteen minutes later, the chainsaw suffocated, chewed in place. In the new-made silence Nat told Aiche that Aiche owed him, he'd saved him a walk back to Browning, those fifteen minutes of gas wouldn't have reached halfway to Babb. But still: he talked from the darkness.

At the beginning of the month-long week-end the stock of the 30.06 wasn't cracked, either, but that was already puttied full, then brushed over with Lin's clear fingernail polish. Practically varnished. Deaner, Aiche's brother, would never know, or, never have to. Unless he fired the gun himself—cracking the putty—and then tried to slide it across a seatcover. But there were no deer or elk in the streets of Great Falls, and Deaner was doing his best low-profile anyway, moving from empty house to empty house—houses he was supposed to be selling with his broker's license, the owners in places like Texas and California and jail. Over the phone Deaner calls it payback and considers himself a hero, a homesteader.

By the first stoplight of Great Falls Aiche has the *Tribune* laid out on the seat, classifieds up, held open by the 30.06. New coffee steaming on the dash. Nat's wooly-eared hat pulled down low against the morning cold, against identification. Under REAL ESTATE Deaner is a shit-grinning profile on the photocopy of a coin—Montana Property Services—and there are four three-bedroom/two-bath unfurnished homes he could be sleeping late in, two of them with garages. Because Deaner's Monte Carlo is distinctive—the same Candy Apple as Aiche's truck, painted the same afternoon even—Aiche suspects the homes with garages, falls in behind a school bus groaning up the hill into the residential he needs.

He can tell he's getting closer to Deaner.

Through the windowsteam of his coffee the lights on the rear end of the schoolbus pony back and forth, back and forth, and Aiche drinks, and he won't pass, even when the schoolbus anticipates his next right. Better to err on the side of the law, watch the mothers bowl the kids out their front doors to the bus stop. The second mother leans forward from her robe, waving at Aiche or at the truck maybe, and Aiche allows his hand to place the coffee back on the dash in what could be taken as a wave back. Whoever she is. By the bus' fourth rolling stop Aiche is talking himself patient, and then there's another wave from another stooped robe and Aiche raises the collar on his coveralls, burrows in, keeps it in second gear. Laughs: maybe Deaner has a kid now, and the bus is going right to him, a big yellow dog leading Aiche by the arm. A thousand pounds of kid in there easy. The eighth stop is for some Indian kids but the mother doesn't wave, but doesn't huddle back in either. Instead watches Aiche groan by in second, shakes her head at him in disapproval. The ninth stop is where it happens, a house with a garage and a couple of snows built up in the driveway.

Aiche doesn't see the two blond kids bail off the porch yet, into the wind, running. He doesn't see because the house is built on a hill and the bus after it stops rolls backwards, and Aiche is easing off the brake, rolling with it, holding onto his coffee, not seeing the blond boy and his big sister miss the bus completely, veer behind it, and by the time they cease being peripheral for Aiche it's too late, they've already beelined his passenger door that doesn't lock. The girl wrenches it open and the boy crawls up, in, her following, Aiche still holding his coffee level against the slant he's on, they're on, all disguised against the cold. Past them on the porch is a sandy-haired mother, squinting, waving, and Aiche waves back, for help, but then the girl pulls the door to, closing the three of them in, fumbling across the boy for the heater controls.

'It doesn't work,' Aiche says, and then the boy shifts into second with both hands and Aiche eases off the clutch—a reflex—pulls away, doesn't answer when the boy asks where the plow is, are they going to get it first? As the boy shifts them into third, the bus already disappeared, Aiche looks over at the girl and she looks back at him with narrowing eyes, and then back to the row her house is part of.

This is how it happens.

"You're Indian," she says. Maybe nine years old.

"Blackfeet."

"You're not Uncle Jay."

"No. More like Uncle Aiche"'

The boy looks up at Aiche. Aiche smiles. "I guess I'm your ride, today, too."

The girl says Aiche isn't a real name and Aiche doesn't say neither is Jay, instead asks back which school they go to. No answer. The bus is probably picking up Deaner's non-kid right about now, and there's probably a hundred other normal things happening too. Aiche asks why don't they ride the bus and this gets a question back, from the boy: "This your gun?" Aiche nods, moves it to his other side, which isn't easy, the sling and scope catching on everything, the girl flattened against the passenger door. Aiche corrects himself, says it's not really his.

"Then what are you doing with it?" the girl asks, in what has to be her mother's voice, and as Aiche triangulates in on where he remembers a basketball court being that might have had a school by it five years ago he tells them about Deaner, about the moose and the chainsaw, about Nat bugging him all the time. Makes the *bzz* noise, slapping his collared neck. The boy accidentally laughs; his big sister shushes him. A stop sign stealths up and the defunct defrost vents drink unexpected coffee, wake up enough to cough steam for the first time ever.

Aiche pats the dash and doesn't turn on the radio because he doesn't want to be a description on it. Better to just drop the kids off as Uncle Jay might, find Deaner, get the Minute Rice for Lin that they don't carry at the Browning IGA, and then skulk out of town, limp home. Maybe paint the truck blue next summer, or even two-tone it if Nat'll help tape. Aiche realizes too late that he's telling all this to the kids, tries to correct, cover. "I'm not really Blackfeet," he says. "Navajo."

"You're nervous," the girl says. "Is that a kind of Indian?"

Aiche nods, nods, and the next corner opens onto the basketball goal from his memory, the rim bent down now and an elementary school beautiful and glorious all around, brick and crayon, letters and monkeybars. The boy downshifts for the drop-off lane, and Aiche complies with his clutch leg, noses in behind a mini-van. Slows to a stop when it's his turn. The girl opens the door, stands there looking into the cab, her head level with the bench seat.

"You're going to get in trouble for this," she says.

Aiche waves bye to her, tells her to have a good day, but then the boy is still there. Aiche doesn't understand; the big sister explains: "He's not old enough for real school, yet. Only I am. He goes to the other one."

Before Aiche can say it—the other one?—she's closed the door, is putting on her nojoke elementary school demeanor, her backpack slung proper over both shoulders. Going to find a phone maybe, or a teacher, a principal, God. Aiche pushes the boy gently towards the passenger door. Behind them mothers late for work are applying make-up, leaning on their horns.

"You can go to this one today," Aiche says, but the boy shakes his head no.

"This one isn't mine," he says, and is already in his sister's abandoned seat, reaching for the lap belt, pulling on the chainsaw pullcord until Aiche leans over, secures him right. They look long at each other and finally Aiche tells the boy okay and satisfies the eight-to-fivers behind him, pulls back into Great Falls as if he's ever known where a preschool is or what one might look like.

He can feel himself pulling farther and farther away from Deaner.

He makes small-talk with the boy, who for an address offers "the big house with all the stairs." Coffee might help, a local clerk. And Minute-Rice is still on the list, for Lin. If the FBI doesn't swoop down on him out of the sky. For legal purposes he tells the boy in as many ways as he can that he's not kidnapping him. The boy says he knows, he's been kidnapped once already, by his dad.

"Your dad?"

"He's in Arizona."

"Did he take you there?"

"No. We went to a hotel and watched cartoons and then called Mom."

"You know your phone number, don't you?"

The boy nods, repeats it rote, tags on his address for good measure. Aiche smiles, asks the boy how he'd like to just go home today, skip school? The boy shrugs, looks once at Aiche and then away. "The one with the Manimals," he says.

"What?"

"Our cartoon."

"Oh."

"They have guns, too. Uncle Jay has a plow."

Aiche agrees, makes more small talk, listens to the formula of the cartoon the boy watched in the hotel: how there's always a kid in the kind of complicated trouble only a direct animal approach can get him out of. The bus passes them going the other way and the bus driver stares Aiche down, and Aiche stares back. The boy turns in his seat and watches the bus recede. He tells Aiche to tell him about his bug-friend and Aiche does, tells about Nat the time he broke his foot from trying to run in two kinds of different boots, tells about when Nat was going to get rich selling doggie-doors on the reservation—because it made sense: there were so many dogs. But no one wanted all of them in the house, yeah? The boy laughs and Aiche too, because it's half a lie, and the next stop sign is leaning from the parking lot of a convenience store. Aiche asks the boy is it's all right, and when it is, he pulls in, leaves the truck running, gets to the door before he remembers the 30.06, how the boy's been watching it. He stifflegs it back.

In the cab the boy is doing nothing, his feet not quite making the floor. Aiche reaches in, slings the gun over a shoulder and tells the kid just to wait for a half second, cool? The boy nods, swings his feet, says it—"Cool"—which is the opposite of the mood in the convenience store, even after Aiche lays the gun on the counter. The clerk doesn't touch it. Aiche piles all the Minute- Rices there are on top, along with two coffees.

"They're yours," the clerk says, hands visible.

Aiche shakes his head no, in disbelief, but the clerk is nodding yes, taking note of the blonde kid watching this thing unfold. Aiche can see it, the way he's holding his lips in pre-witness mode.

"This isn't a robbery," Aiche says.

"And you're not a kidnapper either," the clerk says back, "I know the drill, man. I've been around, shit. Just take it easy."

"I'm trying to."

Aiche leaves six and half dollars on the counter and then backs the truck all the way out to the street, trying to keep his license plate hidden. For what it's worth. By the time they reach the boy's street, the familiar row of houses, they're both drinking coffee. Aiche says it's what Nervous Indians drink, and the boy smiles into his cup, with the curving styrofoam rim, and is frozen like that in the side-glass as they pass his house they meant to stop at, Uncle Jay's red truck plowed through the drive-way snow, Uncle Jay a large man in the yard, consoling the mother, still in her robe. The only motion is head motion, the only sound Aiche's engine, snow crunching, the truck slowing indecisively and then decisively not slowing. Explanations wholly unformed, a lump in the throat. Soon enough, the mother losing her house moccasins as she flits across the yard, after Aiche, Uncle Jay diving for his truck, the plow dragging sparks across the drive as he bounces out, his weight carrying him into the neighbor across the street's yard, which is soft, needy.

In Aiche's rearview Uncle Jay is out locking his hubs, dropping the plow, and Aiche is careful not to speed because speeding people don't blend well. He climbs the hill, deeper into residential. Below, at an intersection, Uncle Jay's truck, a siren magneted on top, his headlights switching back and forth. Aiche looks at the boy, asks. "He a police man?"

"Fireman."

Aiche nods, takes smaller and smaller sidestreets, until he's leaving new tracks in the road, the first one out this morning. The 30.06 is nosed behind the accelerator again. When the boy asks if he can shift Aiche says maybe later, not now. The boy asks then where are they going, and Aiche has no answer; Pre-school is still an address in the yellow pages he didn't tear out, didn't even ask the clerk for. The big house with all the stairs. "Up," he says, more to himself, "up." At least he got Lin's rice. And paid for it. That's one thing. The next is the realtor sign in the yard of the house streaming by. Not Deaner's—Montana Property Services—but an idea. They're in the right block numbers, anyway, for the two garage homes. Aiche takes all the roads, the names slurring together, the gas gauge diving too deep to be coming to a complete stop at every intersection.

The first Montana Property Services house has yellow shutters and brings canaries to mind. Aiche idles outside, and finally—with the 30.06—trudges up to the garage, cups his hands to see through the glass: cardboard boxes and a broken washing machine. No candy apple Monte Carlo. No Deaner. A mother on the porch across the street, evidently locked out since the bus run. Aiche stares at her until there's a distant trucksound, and then he steps behind the fenceless house, follows a trellis onto the roof, kneels at the highest place, looking through the scope at the road that got him here—nothing—then sweeping wider and wider, until the mother across the street is pinned to her front door, already preparing her re-creation of the Indian silhouette she'll draw for the morning *Tribune*, adding the bandana herself. Aiche holds the rifle up, out, but she'll take words to calm down. If anything. He slides down, nods to the boy as he passes, tells him with a finger just one more minute. Scans windows for potential witnesses. From a safe distance he asks the mother if she knows that boy's parents maybe, or just his mother? Finds himself explaining about the Arizona father, apologizing for him almost. The mother answers by crumbling against the wall, holding herself against the cold. "Ma'am," Aiche says, "now this is important. Do you know him?" She looks to the truck, to the boy watching, and says simply "What's his name, then?" Aiche realizes then that the boy is nameless. Down the hill the sound of a truck, too. Already. In two steps he's at the mother's door with the butt of the rifle. It's hollow core for some reason; the door gives before the lock, and Aiche reaches in, undoes that. Leaves. Behind him the blue-lipped woman calls out thank you, thank you, but Aiche can't look back, is busy hiding in his upturned collar. In the truck the boy notices the crack reopened on the stock. "She broke your gun," he says, and Aiche nods, heads to the next house Deaner might be. This time he pulls right up in the driveway, and isn't even out of gear before the automatic garage door begins rising for him like salvation, Deaner's car there to the left. Deaner. Aiche pulls forward, in, but the truck's too tall, the visor at cave-level. He closes his eyes, opens them, looks to the boy and then rolls back, turns around, backs in as deep as he can, covers the hood with a tarp, holding it in place with the wipers.

Deaner is waiting for them in the kitchen when they finally make it in, the boy in tow. A barely unfolded card table and some peach crates. Deaner turns his scanner down for the moment, is indirect: "So how's the wood hawking, then?"

"Dry," Aiche says, a halfjoke. "Meet Bill Martinson, Billy to his friends."

Deaner shakes the boy's hands importantly, telling him in a wooden Indian voice to remember all this, his captivity, then thumbs the scanner back up. On it Uncle Jay is talking to some patrolman, repeating where he is, where he isn't. Deaner explains: the officers keep converging on Jay, on his red truck. Exasperation is the name of the game. Aiche smiles, collapses on a crate. Billy Martinson stands so that his jacket is in contact with Aiche's overalls. Deaner nods to Aiche about Billy

Martinson.

"So you're taking hostages already?"

"I'm taking him to his school."

"And I thought I was the only hostile in the family."

Aiche shrugs, tells him he still is the only one. He only wants to get back, go home. Deaner reminds him about the convenience store, and, before Aiche can explain, says it would have made more sense to take the kid in, right? Leave the gun in the truck?

"But that door doesn't lock," Aiche says.

"This isn't Browning, H, shit. It takes them longer to steal it up here. Have to get their balls together, justify it beforehand." He stands, walks around Billy Martinson and Aiche. Touches Billy Martinson's shoulder so that Billy Martinson flinches away.

"You're scaring him," Aiche says, a warning.

Deaner stares at Aiche for too long, says it: that Aiche could have left the kid on any corner. Aiche shakes his head no, and they leave it at that. "I broke and entered too, I guess," he says. "For this lady."

Deaner shakes his head, asks how long has Aiche been in town, again?

"Too long," Aiche says. "I just need to get out of here, leave the kid with somebody he knows."

"Because—"

"Because he's a kid, Dee. This isn't his fault. Mistaken identity. His dad's in Arizona."

"And you're here."

"It's not like that."

"Like what, H? Who's the hostage here? Remind me now."

Aiche looks purposefully out the window and in the inattention Deaner smiles the kid over, after a few false starts tells him how his little brother Aiche is a wolf to the park rangers, tolerated because he keeps the elk herd thin enough so they don't starve. Asks the kid what he wants to be, someday.

The kid shrugs a kid shrug, Aiche's shrug.

"You're scaring him," Aiche says. "He doesn't understand."

"Shhh," Deaner says, smiling. "I'm making a first impression here. After this he's going to grow up and tell people about you, about me. Like it really is. But not until then, right? After the statutes?"

Billy Martinson looks to Aiche and Aiche nods, so he does too.

Deaner says now that we've got that settled, and then they sit, listen to Uncle Jay cuss the police over the scanner. They know now that Aiche is Indian, probably Flathead, truck registered in a woman's name, possibly stolen. Deaner says Aiche is a wolf alright, for real now, and white people shoot wolves that come to town, ba bam bam bam. Don't want them raising their little ones. He says it for Aiche. Aiche shakes his head and ignores, repeats: "I need to get out of here."

"And I need a couch," Deaner says. "What do you need, Bill Martinson?"

Billy Martinson doesn't say anything, just looks at the dead television set. Aiche fills in: "Cartoons."

"A little vitamin TV, yeah?"

Billy Martinson won't nod for Deaner, though. Aiche says maybe they could trade vehicles, but Deaner says no, you ride out on the horse you rode in on.

"Why?"

"Because it sounds right."

"Well at least I can leave the thirty-aught-six."

Deaner shakes his head no again, though: the rifle's a weapon now, potential evidence A gift. Aiche thanks him, asks if he's going to be any help at all. Deaner smiles his evilest smile, then says he's still the big brother, here. And this is just Great Falls, after all. They can counter jurisdiction with distraction, draw the cops and the firemen to one side of town, let Aiche slip out the other.

"A distraction?" Aiche asks.

Deaner nods.

"What about him, Billy?"

"Leave him with me."

Aiche looks down at Billy Martinson, and Billy Martinson is paler than he was before, his lower lip trembling, bitten. His hand grips the extra of Aiche's jeans, and Aiche places his hand over Billy Martinson's. He shakes his head no to Deaner, an apology.

"So what's your distraction, then?" he asks, but is interrupted by the scanner, a patrolman whispering for some reason through the static. About an empty house with a truck backed halfway into the garage, tarped down. The advice he gets from Uncle Jay is to circle, wait, the Indian is his, don't flush him out. Deaner looks to Aiche and Aiche stands, exhales, nods once. "Do it already," he says, "distract them if you can."

"I can."

"It's all downhill from here, right?"

Deaner nods.

"You got any gas in the garage?"

Deaner smiles one side of his face. "Damn Indians," he says, "money in their pocket and they'll still run out of gas."

"Like we ran out of grass."

It's something historical between them, drugs or land. They're brothers. In the garage just after the patrolman's second unobvious drive-by they siphon from the Monte Carlo to the truck, by way of a bucket because the hose isn't quite long enough. Gas sloshes everywhere. Aiche seatbelts Billy Martinson in, walks around the bed of the truck, doesn't need to say bye to Deaner, the hose still sticking out the side of his Monte Carlo, the siphon not all the way broken. Deaner says to Aiche to tell Lin hey, and that other one, and then he depockets a worn Manimal toy, says his clients left it.

"Where are they now?" Aiche asks, complicit.

Deaner shrugs, gestures wide, enough to mean back overseas, closes the motion by handing the Manimal through the window, Aiche passing it on to Billy Martinson. Deaner says in his wooden Indian voice again that it's an Indian gift, don't forget it, and then Aiche is letting the truck roll back, cutting it sharp at the end of the driveway, waiting for their weight to take them downhill, start the truck for them. The 30.06 ran down the side of his leg, the truck gathering speed, starting in third even, the patrolmen unaware, creeping up on the tarp dragged four houses down and then left blowing.

Browning is four hours away, ten minutes of that town, five of that ten residential, and in residential, some six stopsigns to slide through. At the second the near collision is a house, because they have to make the downhill turn, and at the fourth the near collision is another red truck, Uncle Jay. Billy Martinson doesn't wave, has his feet on the dash. The locked hubs of Uncle Jay's truck pop violently as he u-turns in the rearview, and he never turns the light on. Meaning it'll be personal. The gun rack behind his head gunless.

Aiche starts laughing and is scared of his voice.

Billy Martinson smiling, Manimaled, living out a cartoon, Minute Rice circulating freely through the cab.

Aiche can feel Uncle Jay getting closer.

Town slips by in greys and disinterested faces, and then the trucks are stretching out on the floor of what Aiche tells Billy

Martinson he thinks used to be Prickly Pear Valley, a long time ago. Billy Martinson watches the yellow grass whip by. asks how long ago, and Aiche look with him, out to where the grass is still in relation to them, a fixed point.

"About eighty years," he says, finally, and somehow the nearness of it takes his weight off the accelerator, and his truck coasts to a stop, pulled across the road, blocking it, Uncle Jay a mirror image fifty yards closer to Great Falls. Candy Apple and Fire Engine red, motionless, no other traffic. Aiche tells Billy Martinson he's sorry, and then the wood stock of the gun is in his hand.

Billy Martinson asks Aiche if he's going to turn into a wolf now.

Aiche looks at him, doesn't laugh. Says it: "Yeah." From Uncle Jay's disadvantage point behind the rifle eased into the V of his door and cab all there can be is a Flathead Indian, a rifle, a stolen truck and a nephew kidnapped at gunpoint. Motion in the cab, for too long, and then the door opening, the nephew on the Indian's knees, the Indian holding the rifle barrel up, its butt against hipbone.

They step down as one.

The Indian keeps the rifle well away from his body, the nephew on his other arm. Allowing no excuses. He stares at Jay, says something which doesn't carry, and then sends the nephew walking over, looking back once and getting waved on for it. Whatever the Indian's saying, he says it again, and this time points, back up the hill on the other side of Great Falls, where a Montana Property Services three-bedroom/two-bath unfurnished home is burning, great plumes of black smoke billowing up like an insurance settlement. They all stare and wait for something to explode and while waiting one of them drives silently north on two gallons of siphoned gas.

Aiche Teasley. Blackfeet Indian, Piegan, Pikuni. At twenty-seven he had child he never talked about, or only talked about with Nat, a child who lived with his mother, was the reason Aiche refused to get a job, because alimony would just garnish his check away. He died four years after he shared the front page of the *Tribune* with a many-alarm fire, when his now-blue and silver truck rolled into Landslide, either killing two deer with his front bumper and then field dressing them on the way down or spilling those deer from his bed as he rolled. Fifteen years after the facts his child he didn't support with money tells it the first way, like he killed the deer on the way down, aimed for them because his gun caught on the seatcover at the exact wrong moment, clanging into the action figure hanging from the visor and spooking the deer he refused to let bound away. The last time anybody remembers him leaving the reservation was when he went to Great Falls and ran out of gas trying to get out, pre-described, two highway patrols converging on him, unable in the end to charge him with anything worth the ride back into town because the 30.06 he'd carried onto school grounds and then used on a convenience store clerk had no shells the troopers could find, shells they begged and bargained existence for, tried to dig out of ashtrays and door panels and headliners and every other possible place except for the pockets of my school jeans as I walked from one red truck to another, moving between letters, the smoke marking my return, leading me deeper into town than I ever wanted to go.

The Derelict

E. Pauline Johnson

Cragstone had committed what his world called a crime—an inexcusable offence that caused him to be shunned by society and estranged from his father's house. He had proved a failure.

Not one of his whole family connections could say unto the others, "I told you so," when he turned out badly.

They had all predicted that he was born for great things, then to discover that they had overestimated him was irritating, it told against their discernment, it was unflattering, and they thought him inconsiderate.

So, in addition to his failure, Cragstone had to face the fact that he had made himself unpopular among his kin.

As a boy, he had been the pride of his family, as a youth, its hope of fame and fortune; he was clever, handsome, inventive, original, everything that society and his kind admired, but he criminally fooled them and their expectations, and they never forgave him for it.

He had dabbled in music, literature, law, everything—always with semi-success and brilliant promise; he had even tried the stage, playing the Provinces for an entire season; then, ultimately sinking into mediocrity in all these occupations, he returned to London, a hopelessly useless, a pitiably gifted man. His chilly little aristocratic mother always spoke of him as "poor, dear Charles."

His brothers, clubmen all, graciously alluded to him with, "deuced hard luck, poor Charlie." His father never mentioned his name.

Then he went into "The Church," sailed for Canada, idled about for a few weeks, when one of the great colonial bishops, not knowing what else to do with him, packed him off north as a missionary to the Indians.

And, after four years of disheartening labor amongst a semi-civilized people, came this girl Lydia into his life. This girl of the mixed parentage, the English father, who had been swept northward with the rush of lumber trading, the Chippewa mother, who had been tossed to his arms by the tide of circumstances. The girl was a strange composition of both, a type of mixed blood, pale, dark, slender, with the slim hands, the marvellously beautiful teeth of her mother's people, the ambition, the small tender mouth, the utter fearlessness of the English race. But the strange, laughless eyes, the silent step, the hard sense of honor, proclaimed her far more the daughter of red blood than of white.

And, with the perversity of his kind, Cragstone loved her; he meant to marry her because he knew that he should not. What a monstrous thing it would be if he did! He, the shepherd of this half-civilized flock, the modern John Baptist; he, the voice of the great Anglican Church crying in this wilderness, how could he wed with this Indian girl who had been a common serving-maid in a house in Penetanguishene, and been dismissed therefrom with an accusation of theft that she could never prove untrue? How could he bring this reproach upon the Church? Why, the marriage would have no precedent; and yet he loved her, loved her sweet, silent ways, her listening attitudes, her clear, brown, consumptive-suggesting skin. She was the only thing in all the irksome mission life that had responded to him, had encouraged him to struggle anew for the spiritual welfare of this poor red race. Of course, in Penetanguishene they had told him she was irreclaimable, a thief, with ready lies to cover her crimes; for that very reason he felt tender towards her, she was so sinful, so pathetically human.

He could have mastered himself, perhaps, had she not responded, had he not seen the laughless eyes laugh alone for him, had she not once when a momentary insanity possessed them both confessed in words her love for him as he had done to her. But now? Well, now only this horrible tale of theft and untruth hung between them like a veil; now even with his arms locked about her, his eyes drowned in hers, his ears caught the whispers of calumny, his thoughts were perforated with the horror of his Bishop's censure, and these things rushed between his soul and hers, like some bridgeless deep he might not cross, and so his lonely life went on.

And then one night his sweet humanity, his grand, strong love rose up, battled with him, and conquered. He cast his pharisaical ideas, and the Church's "I am better than thou," aside forever; he would go now, to-night, he would ask her to be his wife, to have and to hold from this day forward, for better, for worse, for—

A shadow fell across the doorway of his simple home; it was August Beaver, the trapper, with the urgent request that he would come across to French Island at once, for old "Medicine Joe" was there, dying, and wished to see the minister. At another time Cragstone would have felt sympathetic, now he was only irritated; he wanted to find Lydia, to look in her laughless eyes, to feel her fingers in his hair, to tell her he did not care if she were a hundred times a thief, that he loved her, loved her, loved her, and he would marry her despite the Church, despite—

"Joe, he's near dead, you come now?" broke in August's voice. Cragstone turned impatiently, got his prayer-book, followed the trapper, took his place in the canoe, and paddled in silence up the bay.

The moon arose, large, limpid, flooding the cabin with a wondrous light, and making more wan the features of a dying man, whose fever-wasted form lay on some lynx skins on the floor.

Cragstone was reading from the *Book of Common Prayer* the exquisite service of the Visitation of the Sick. Outside, the loons clanged up the waterways, the herons called across the islands, but no human things ventured up the wilds. Inside, the sick man lay, beside him August Beaver holding a rude lantern, while Cragstone's matchless voice repeated the Anglican formula. A spasm, an uplifted hand, and Cragstone paused. Was the end coming even before a benediction? But the dying man was addressing Beaver in Chippewa, whispering and choking out the words in his death struggle.

"He says he's bad man," spoke Beaver. A horrible, humorous sensation swept over Cragstone; he hated himself for it, but at college he had always ridiculed death-bed confessions; but in a second that feeling had vanished, he bent his handsome, fair face above the copper- colored countenance of the dying man. "Joe," he said, with that ineffable tenderness that had always drawn human hearts to him, "Joe, tell me before I pronounce the Absolution, how have you been bad? "

"I steal three times," came the answer. "Once horses, two of them from farmer near Barrie. Once twenty fox-skins at North Bay; station man he in jail for those fox-skins now. Once gold watch from doctor at Penetanguishene."

The prayer-book rattled from Cragstone's hands and fell to the floor.

"Tell me about this watch," he mumbled. "How did you come to do it?"

"I liffe at the doctor's, I take care his horse, long time; old River's gal, Lydia, she work there too; they say she steal it; I sell to trader, the doctor he never know, he think Lydia."

Cragstone was white to the lips. "Joe," he faltered, "you are dying; do you regret this sin, are you sorry?"

An indistinct "yes" was all; death was claiming him rapidly.

But a great, white, purified love had swept over the young clergyman. The girl he worshipped could never now be a reproach to his calling, she was proved blameless as a baby, and out of his great human love arose the divine calling, the Christ-like sense of forgiveness, the God-like forgetfulness of injury and suffering done to his and to him, and once more his soft, rich voice broke the stillness of the Northern night, as the Anglican absolution of the dying fell from his lips in merciful tenderness:

"O Lord Jesus Christ, who hath left power to His Church to absolve all sinners who truly repent and believe in Him, of His great mercy forgive thee thine offences, and by His authority committed to me I absolve thee from all thy sins in the name of the Father, and of the Son, and of the Holy Ghost. Amen."

Beaver was holding the lantern close to the penitent's face; Cragstone, kneeling beside him, saw that the end had come already, and, after making the sign of the Cross on the dead

Indian's forehead, the young priest arose and went silently out into the night.

*   *   *

The sun was slipping down into the far horizon, fretted by the inimitable wonder of islands that throng the Georgian Bay; the blood-colored skies, the purpling clouds, the extravagant beauty of a Northern sunset hung in the west like the trailing robes of royalty, soundless in their flaring, their fading; soundless as the unbroken wilds which lay bathed in the loneliness of a dying day.

But on the color-flooded shore stood two, blind to the purple, the scarlet, the gold, blind to all else save the tense straining of the other's eyes; deaf to nature's unsung anthem, hearing only the other's voice. Cragstone stood transfixed with consternation. The memory of the past week of unutterable joy lay blasted with the awfulness of this moment, the memory of even that first day—when he had stood with his arms about her, had told her how he had declared her reclaimed name far and wide, how even Penetanguishene knew now that she had suffered blamelessly, how his own heart throbbed suffocatingly with the honor, the delight of being the poor means through which she had been righted in the accusing eyes of their little world, and that now she would be his wife, his sweet, helping wife, and she had been great enough not to remind him that he had not asked her to be his wife until her name was proved blameless, and he was great enough not to make excuse of the resolve he had set out upon just when August Beaver came to turn the current of his life.

But he had other eyes to face to-night, eyes that blurred the past, that burned themselves into his being—the condemning, justly and righteously indignant eyes of his Bishop—while his numb heart, rather than his ears, listened to the words that fell from the prelate's lips like curses on his soul, like the door that would shut him forever outside the holy place.

"What have you done, you pretended servant of the living God? What use is this you have made of your Holy Orders? You hear the confessions of a dying man, you absolve and you bless him, and come away from the poor dead thief to shout his crimes in the ears of the world, to dishonor him, to be a discredit to your calling. Who could trust again such a man as you have proved to be faithless to himself, faithless to his Church, faithless to his God?"

But Cragstone was on the sands at his accuser's feet. "Oh! my lord," he cried, "I meant only to save the name of a poor, mistrusted girl, selfishly, perhaps, but I would have done the same thing just for humanity's sake had it been another to whom injustice was done."

"Your plea of justice is worse than weak; to save the good name of the living is it just to rob the dead?"

The Bishop's voice was like iron.

"I did not realize I was a priest, I only knew I was a man," and with these words Cragstone arose and looked fearlessly, even proudly, at the one who stood his judge.

"Is it not better, my lord, to serve the living than the dead?"

"And bring reproach upon your Church?" said the Bishop, sternly.

It was the first thought Cragstone ever had of his official crime; he staggered under the horror of it, and the little, dark, silent figure, that had followed them unseen, realized in her hiding amid the shadows that the man who had lifted her into the light was himself being thrust down into irremediable darkness. But Cragstone only saw the Bishop looking at him as from a supreme height, he only felt the final stinging lash in the words: "When a man disregards the most sacred offices of his God, he will hardly reverence the claims of justice of a simple woman who knows not his world, and if he so easily flings his God away for a woman, just so easily will he fling her away for other gods."

And Lydia, with eyes that blazed like flame, watched the Bishop turn and walk frigidly up the sands, his indignation against this outrager of the Church declaring itself in every foot-fall.

Cragstone flung himself down, burying his face in his hands. What a wreck he had made of life! He saw his future, loveless, for no woman would trust him now; even the one whose name he had saved would probably be more unforgiving than the Church; it was the way with women when a man abandoned God and honor for them; and this nameless but blackest of sins, this falsity to one poor dying sinner, would stand between him and heaven forever, though through that very crime he had saved a fellow being. Where was the justice of it?

The purple had died from out the western sky, the waters of the Georgian Bay lay colorless at his feet, night was covering the world and stealing with inky blackness into his soul.

She crept out of her hiding-place, and, coming, gently touched his tumbled fair hair; but he shrank from her, crying: "Lydia, my girl, my girl, I am not for a good woman now! I, who thought you an outcast, a thief, not worthy to be my wife, tonight I am not an outcast of man alone, but of God."

But what cared she for his official crimes? She was a woman. Her arms were about him, her lips on his; and he who had, until now, been a portless derelict, who had vainly sought a haven in art, an anchorage in the service of God, had drifted at last into the world's most sheltered harbor—a woman's love.

But, of course, the Bishop took away his gown.

THE CONTRIBUTORS

SALLI BENEDICT - Born in 1954, Salli Benedict holds degrees in Visual Arts and Native Studies. An Awkesasne Mohawk, she currrently lives on the Akwesasne Reservation in upstate New York, where she has been director of the Akwesasne Museum. She is the author of several Mohawk language textbooks.

GLORIA BIRD - A member of the Spokane Tribe of Washington State, Gloria Bird's book *Full Moon on the Reservation* won the Diane Decorah First Book Award for Poetry. She has co-edited with Joy Harjo the anthology *Reinventing the Enemy's Language: North American Native Women's Writing*. An associate editor for the *Wicazo Sa Review*, she currently lives in Spokane, Washington.

PETER BLUE CLOUD - A member of the Turtle Clan, Mohawk Nation, Peter Blue Cloud/Aroniawenrate was born at Caughnawaga Reserve in Quebec in 1927. Recipient of an

American Book Award, he is a poet, carpenter and wood carver, and former editor of *Akwesasne Notes*. His publications include *White Corn Sister, Elderberry Flute Song: Contemporary Coyote Tales, The Other Side of Nowhere*, and *Clans of Many Nations: Selected Poems 1969–1994*.

KIMBERLY M. BLAESER - An enrolled member of the Minnesota Chippewa Tribe, Kimberly M. Blaeser grew up on the White Earth Reservation in northwestern Minnesota. Her publications include *Trailing You*, which won the Diane Decorah First Book Award for Poetry from the Native Writer's Circle of the Americas, and *Gerald Vizenor: Writing in the Oral Tradition*, a critical study. She is associate professor of English at the University of Wisconsin-Milwaukee.

DWAYNE LESLIE BOWEN - A Seneca, Dwayne Leslie Bowen is the author of one collection, *One More Story and Others*, published by the Greenfield Review Press.

JOSEPH BRUCHAC - An Abnacki writer and storyteller, Joseph Bruchac and his wife Carol live in the same house in the Adirondack foothills town of Greenfield Center, New York, where his was raised by his grandparents. His published works include *Bowman's Store*, an autobiography published in 1997, *Between Earth and Sky: Legends of Native American Sacred Places*, and *The Boy Who Lived With Bears and Other Iroquois Stories*.

MARIA CAMPBELL - Born in 1940 in Saskatchewan, Canada, Maria Campbell grew up in a home where Cree rituals were practiced alongside Catholic ceremony. Her autobiography, *Halfbreed*, details the tribulations her mixed family endured.

Her other published works include *Little Badger and the Fire People, People of the Buffalo: How the Plains Indians Lived*, and *Achimoona*.

ROBERT J. CONLEY - Author of moe than twenty novels, most recently *War Woman*, as well as numerous stories and poems, Robert J. Conley is Cherokee. A three-time winner of the Spur Award, he lives in Tahlequah, Oklahoma. His published works include *Incident at Buffalo Crossing, Mountain Windsong: A Novel of the Trail of Tears*, and *The Witch of Goingsnake and Other Stories*.

ELIZABETH COOK-LYNN - Of Crow Creek Sioux ancestry, Elizabeth Cook-Lynn lives in a log home at the confluence of the Spokane and Columbia Rivers. She has been professor of Indian Studies at Eastern Washington University. Her published work includes *The Badger Said This* and *Seek the House of Relatives*.

RAY FADDEN/TEHANETORENS - A master storyteller in the Mohawk tradition, Ray Fadden's book, *Legends of the Iroquois*, was presented in pictograph form with English translation. He lives in the Adirondack Mountains in New York State.

ERIC GANSWORTH - Born and raised on the Tuscarora Indian Reservation in Western New York, Eric Gansworth is an Onondaga. His first novel, *Indian Summers*, was published by Michigan State University Press in 1998. His work has appeared in numerous anthologies and journals. Also a painter and photographer, his work has been shown in a number of exhibits. He is a member of the English faculty at Niagara County Community College in Niagara Falls, New York.

JOY HARJO - Born in Tulsa, Oklahoma in 1951, Joy Harjo is Creek. She received a B.A. from the University of New Mexicvo and an M.F.A. from the Iowa Writers Workshop. She has taught at both the Institute of American Indian Art and Arizona State University. Her books include *A Map of the Next World*, *The Woman Who Fell From the Sky*, and *She Had Some Horses*. She presently lives in Santa Fe, New Mexico.

INEZ HERNÁNDEZ-AVILA - Of Nimipu (Nez Perce) and Chicana background, Hernández-Avila received a Ph.D. in English fron the University of Houston, Her published works include *Con Razon, Corazon* and *War Dance*.

E. PAULINE JOHNSON - Born in Canada in 1861, E. Pauline Johnson/Tekahionwake was the daughter of a Mohawk chief and an English woman. Her stories describe what it meant to be an Indian in a country conquered by the British. Her books include *Legends of Vancouver* and *The Moccasin Maker*. She died in 1913.

STEPHEN GRAHAM JONES - An enrolled Blackfeet, Stephen Graham Jones has had work published in numerous magazines and journals incluiding *Black Warrior Review, Blood & Ahorisms, Cutbank, Georgetown Review,* and *Phoebe*.

MAURICE KENNY - Winner of an American Book Award for *The Mama Poems*, Maurice Kenny presently lives in Saranac Lake, New York, high in the Adirondacks, and is visiting professor at the State University of New York at Potsdam. His most recent books, both published by the University of Michigan Press, are *Tortured Skins & Other Fictions* and *In the Time of the Present*. His books include *Backward to Forward,* a collection of essays; *Between Two Rivers: Selected Poems; Blackrobe: Isaac Jogues; Tekonwatonti: Molly Brant;* and *Rain & Other Fictions.* His work has appeared in numerous anthologies and has been translated into many other languages, including Russian.

LARRY LITTLEBIRD - Laguna/Santa Domingo writer Larry Littlebird's publised works include *Hunter's Heart.*

EVELINA ZUNI LUCERO - A professor of creative writing at the Institute of American Indian Arts in Santa Fe, New Mexico, Evelina Zuni Lucero is Isleta/San Juan Pueblo. Her short fiction has appeared in numerous journals and anthologies including *Blue Mesa Review, Northeast Indian Quarterly, Cimarron Review,* and *Returning the Gift.*

D'ARCY MCNICKLE - The late D'Arcy McNickle was of Flathead ancerstry. Her published works include *The Surrounded, The Hawk is Hungry and Other Stories,* and *Runner in the Sun: A Story of Indian Maize.*

JOHN C. MOHAWK - A noted Seneca orator and former editor of *Akwesasne Notes,* Mokhawk presently teaches at the University of Buffalo. He lives in Sanborn, New York.

DANIEL DAVID MOSES - Playwright and poet Daniel David Moses is a Delaware from the Six Nations lands along the Grand River in southern Ontario. His plays include *Coyote City, Almighty Voice and His Wife,* and The *Indian Medicine Shows,* for which he won the 1996 James Buller Memorial Award for Excellence in Aboriginal Theatre. His poetry is collected in

Delicate Bodies and *The White Line*. He co-edited, with Terry Goldie, *An Anthology of Canadian Native Literature in English*.

LOUIS LITTLECOON OLIVER - The late Louis Littlecoon Oliver, a full-blood Muskogee/Creek, was born in Koweta Town in 1904, three years before Oklahoma statehood. His first book was not published until his seventh decade, but by the time of his death in 1991, he had four books in print, was translated into a dozen languages, and had been chosen Indian Writer of the Year by the state of Oklahoma.

SIMON J. ORTIZ - Simon Ortiz is of the Acoma Pueblo in New Mexico. His published works include *After and Before the Lightning*, *Men on the Moon: Collected Short Stories*, and *Woven Stone*. He edited *Speaking for the Generations: Native Writers on Writing*. He presently lives in Tucson, Arizona.

ROKWAKO - A Mohawk poet, artist, and linguist, Rokwaho is the author of *Covers*, poetry and pen and ink drawings. A fomer editor of *Akwesasne Notes*, his poetry and art appear in may publications and grace numerous book covers.

WENDY ROSE - An instructor in American Indian Studies at Fresno City College, Fresno, California, Wendy Rose is of Hopi-Miwok ancestry. Author of thirteen books of poetry, she has been an NEA Fellowship recipient and has had her work included in numerous anthologies. Her most recent books are *Bone Dance* and *Now Poof She Is Gone*. She presently lives in the Sierra Nevada foothills near Coarsegold, California.

JUAN RULFO - A Native Mexican, Juan Rulfo's published works

include *The Burning Plain and Other Stories* and *Pedro Paramo*.

A. LAVONNE BROWN RUOFF - Professor emerita of English at the University of Illinois at Chicago, Ruoff is currently interim director of the D'Arcy McNickle Center for American Indian History. Ruoff directed four National Endowment for the Humanities Summer Seminars for College Teachers on American Indian Literature and has received two NEH grants. Her awards include a Lifetime-Achievement Award from the American Book Awards (1998) and selection as the first honoree of the Modern Language Association's Division of American Indian Literatures and the Association for Study of American Indian Literatures (1993). Editor of the American Indian Lives series of the University of Nebraska Press, Ruoff is the author of *American Indian Literatures*, and *Literatures of the American Indian* (for middle- and high-school readers). She has edited the works of S. Alice Callahan, George Copway, and E. Pauline Johnson. With Jerry W. Ward, Jr., she edited *Redefining American Literary History*.

CAROL YAZZI-SHAW - A Navajo, Yazzi-Shaw received her bachelor's degree from the University of New Mexico. Her work appears in numerous anthologies, including *Returning the Gift*. She lives in Albuquerque.

LESLIE MARMON SILKO - Laguna writer Leslie Marmon Silko's published works include *Alamanac of the Dead: A Novel*, *Ceremony*, *Gardens in the Dunes*, and *The Delicacy and Strength of Lace: Letters Between Leslie Marmon Siolko and James Wright*.

LORNE SIMON - Micmac writer Lorne Simon's published works

include *Stones and Switches*. His work has appeared in numerous anthologies, including *Gatherings*.

Luci Tapahonso - Navajo writer Luci Tapahonso's published work includes *Blue Horses Rush In*, *Songs of Shiprock Fair* and *A Breeze Swept Through*.

Drew Hayden Taylor - Presently living in Toronto, Ontario, Canada where he writes commentaries for various news media, A prolific playwright, his work has won numerous awards including the Chalmers Canadian Play Award, and the Canadian Authors Association Literary Award for Best Drama. He has also published a collection of his commentaries, *Funny, You Don't Look Like One: Observations of a Blue-Eyed Ojibway*. He served as artistic director of Native Earth Performing Arts Center from 1994-97.

Gail Tremblay - A writer and artist of Onondaga and Mic Mac ancestry, Gail Tremblay teaches at The Evergreen State College in Olympia, Washington. Her work has been widely anthologized. Her most recent book is *Indian Singing: Poems*.

Anna Lee Walters - Of Otoe/Pawnee ancestry, Anna Lee Walters is a recipient of the Virginia McCormick Scully Award and an American Book Award. Her published works include *Ghost Singer: A Novel*, *Talking Indian: Reflections on Survival and Writing*, *The Spirit of Native America: Beauty and Mysticism in American Indian Art*, and *The Sun is not Merciful*.

James Welch - Born on a Blackfoot reservation in Browning, Montana, James Welch is a graduate of the University of

Montana. Blackfeet/Gros Vendre, his work has appeared in numberous journals and anthologies including the *New Yorker*, *The South Dakota Review*, *Poetry Northwest*, and *New American Review*. His first book of poetry, *Riding the Earthboy, 40*, appeared in 1971. Other published works include *The Indian Lawyer*, *The Death of Jim Loney*, and *Killing Custer: The Battle of Little Bighorn and the Fate of the Plains Indians*.

PHYLLIS WOLF - Assinibone/Ojibwa, Wolf's poetry and fiction appear in many anthologies, including *The Clouds Threw This Light*. She has also published in numerous journals.

TED WILLIAMS - Tuscarora, Williams is the author of the satirical novel *The Reservation*, from which his fiction "Hogart" was taken. He presently lives in North Carolina, where he is writing poetry.

CRAIG S. WOMACK - Craig S. Womack, Oklahoma Creek/Cherokee, teaches Native Studies at the University of Lethbridge in Alberta, Canada. His published work includes the book *Red on Red: Native American Literary Separatism*.